Bruised, But Not Broken:

From Private Pain to Public Victory

Linda G. Hodge

Knowledge Power Books
www.knowledgepowerbooks.com

Copyright by Linda G. Hodge 2017

All rights reserved. No part of this book may be reproduced by any mechanical, photographic, or electronic process, or in the form of a phonographic recording; nor may it be stored in a retrieval system, transmitted, or otherwise copied for public or private use without written permission from the publisher.

ISBN: 978-09981701-7-6
Library of Congress Control Number: 2017940662
Edited by: Angela Scott
Literary Director: Sandra L. Slayton
Front and Back Cover Design: Wendy Aguirre

Published by:

Knowledge Power Books
A Division of Knowledge Power Communications, Inc.
Valencia, CA 91355
www.knowledgepowerbooks.com

Printed in the United States of America

ACKNOWLEDGEMENTS

To all the women in this book who have allowed me to be their voice of courage and hope:
> Your stories have inspired me and painted a vivid picture of the unfailing love of Christ.
> Your transparency was heartfelt.
> Your willingness to share secrets of the dark places of your life will always be revered.
> Your trust in me to articulate your stories, I will never take lightly.
> Your love for others has been spoken.
> Your tears have not been wasted.
> Your decision to put your life on display will make a difference for countless others.
> Your pain has now become your stepping stone.
> Your sorrow has turned to dancing.
> Your courage to be "real" has given hope to the hopeless.
> Your reward is great.
> Your life, once a collection of tragedies, is now a collection of priceless treasures.
> Your ability to have weathered many storms is over.
> Your faith is more than a fact, it is action.
> Your ashes have turned to beauty.

PREFACE

At some point in our lives, we encounter challenging or tragic conditions. For countless people, it's the loss of a parent or child that creates a painful void where alcohol, drugs, and sex become the "welcome" panacea. Others may experience a life-threatening accident or illness, which often leaves them "sinking" in hopelessness. Oftentimes, survivors of unspeakable childhood circumstances carry emotional scars, leaving them psychologically debilitated. For myself, I endured years of both physical and emotional abuse at the hands of my first husband "Joe."

Getting married at eighteen years of age was one of the worst mistakes of my life. And, marrying an abusive, overly-controlling alcoholic only added fuel to the fire. Joe was this super macho type, which I found very enticing and challenging. He made me feel safe, especially since my dad passed away when I was twelve. Consequently, I grew up looking for a protector and hero. Joe carried guns, sold weed, and drank beer all day. He was a womanizer, who never held down a job longer than a month. What's more, the verbal abuse Joe inflicted toward his mom should've been a red flag, indicating what my life would resemble.

For the next seven years, my life rotated on a sphere of continual chaos. The first physical abuse started shortly after we married. A guy asked me to dance at a local nightclub, and I agreed. Immediately upon leaving the dance floor, Joe hurriedly rushed me outside the building. Enraged, he began calling me every degrading name one could imagine. Upon arriving at his mom's home, Joe forced me into the bedroom, where the true torture began. One-after-another, Joe was slapping and punching me.

I only seemed to make matters worse by trying to defend myself. I knew Joe had the upper hand, so I didn't fight mightily. All the while, I was hoping his mom would rescue me at any moment. That never happened. She didn't appear until the gun went off. After reaching for a gun, Joe started pointing it directly towards my face. I heard a shot and was paralyzed from intense fear. My heart was beating fast and erratically. A lump rose in my throat. I didn't know if I had survived the shot.

Apparently, Joe reached for a gun under the bed's mattress and pointed it directly towards my face. Shortly thereafter, I realized the bullet had just missed my head. But, my head was throbbing. While on the bed dodging the gun, I hit the back of my head on the window pane. I was seeing stars and crying out to God.

The remaining years of my marriage didn't get any better as I was becoming more enabled and made to feel like a fool. I was feeling worthless and helpless. Yet, I was caught between having the desire for my marriage to succeed and an awareness it could possibly cost me everything. The price tag of remaining in that relationship was outweighing the need for love.

Eventually, I got the strength to say, "So long!" to the pain.

It's time we girls tell our stories to others. Let's have a chat, you and me, through these pages. I'd be honored if you'd join me and make a difference for others who may have experienced similar situations. Become a voice for the voiceless and hope to the hopeless!

Bruised, But Not Broken: From Private Pain to Public Victory is about real stories and real women, who had once swallowed the poisonous venom of life. Venom is defined as a poisonous substance secreted by animals such as snakes, spiders, and scorpions. This poison is typically injected into prey or aggressors by biting or stinging. Women in these stories were "bitten" by the deadly venom of extreme malice, bitterness, animosity, antagonism, and hostility. On the other hand, perpetrators' extreme malice (venom) was shown in their attitudes, speech, or actions.

Furthermore, when a person is bitten or injected by venom, he is given an antidote. It is a substance which can counteract a form of poisoning. The antidote for particular toxins is manufactured by injecting the toxin into an animal via a small dose and extracting the resulting antibodies from the host animal's blood. This anti-venom can then be used to counteract poison produced by certain species of snakes, spiders, and other venomous animals.

Your memories have become the "antidote" to inform other women of God's grace and to give them a hope and a future. As women, we can sit around like victims and talk about how unfair life has been, or we can choose to become well-equipped and live our best life now.

Bruised, But Not Broken*: *From Private Pain to Public Victory is a book for any woman who courageously chooses to step out of defeat and walk toward victory.

I am the voice of seven women who were unable to write or

verbalize their story. They have decided to unmask their faces, remove the shame, recover from humiliation, and become an instrument of strength and dignity.

Each one has regained her voice. No longer living within their stories, they're now living above their stories. Deliberately, they have decided to no longer put a sexy bandage on their pain. They no longer serve others before serving themselves, saying, "Yes," when they really wanted to say, "No."

Usually, at one time or another while growing up, your crayon may break while coloring. Some may decide to no longer color, while others choose to use the broken crayon and continue coloring their picture. The latter group knows that, even though the crayon is broken, it still works. Therefore, they continue coloring their picture with a broken crayon. Many lives have been broken from choices people made or situations that happened to them. Consequently, they choose to no longer color their picture. Even with a broken life, you can repair it, move forward, and color your world! Pick back up your dreams and begin to place texture and purpose into your life.

Fear of the future makes people settle for things in the present that completely defy abundant life. It also insults the grace of God that He has provided for us. We agonize over how we'll possibly make it, yet all the while, we can glance over our shoulders and see where God has carried us.

Somehow, in some way, every woman's story I share in these pages is a piece of my own story. I may not have experienced every detail of these ladies' journeys, but I'm able to empathize with each one. By the grace and power of God, I've had the exhilarating joy of winning many battles – some of them against no small foes. I've experienced dramatic victory over sexual sin, unhealthy relationships, and other equally fierce opponents. As a survivor of numerous obstacles, I've learned what it takes to rise from a state of "brokenness" into a victorious life! You'll find real-life accounts from survivors who've triumphed over seemingly insurmountable challenges. Equipped with the right tools, you can recover, regroup, and renew your life!

CONTENTS

Acknowledgements v

Preface vii

Chapter 1   My First Kiss 1

Chapter 2   Breaking the Cycle 21

Chapter 3   Worthy of Love 45

Chapter 4   Stolen Innocence 67

Chapter 5   A Stormy Season 83

Chapter 6   Seeing Clearly 101

Chapter 7   Unconditional Love 117

About the Author 137

Chapter 1

"MY FIRST KISS"

As a young child growing up, Sunday mornings always smelled the best. My favorite ruffled dress had the garden-fresh scent of laundry dried on outside clotheslines. I loved the crisp, fresh smell of cotton sliding across my face. Mom's dress was clean, simple, and well-fitted, with perfectly matched accessories. Mom was a fashionista in her collarless dresses and matching jackets with one large top button. She wore sensible low-heel shoes. And on occasion, Mom would sport a trendy hat that accented her stylish attire. Mom was the pastor's wife of our small church, so she had to look and dress the part of a First Lady. Her bouffant hairdo required a lot of hairspray.

When Mom would appear from the restroom, her towering and sweet hair would leave the vivid scent of holding spray. The combined, varying aromas reminded my nose of this favorite day of the week. However, the absolute best Sunday morning smell was the sizzling bacon, which was prepared with eggs, grits, and biscuits and gravy.

After breakfast, we would dash out of the house, Mom asking Dad, "you got your Bible and briefcase?" and, "What about your glasses?" Dad replied back in his authoritarian voice, "Sue May, I've got all my belongings." This dialogue between them both was their habitual conversation prior to stepping foot outside the front door.

The drive crossing from Mississippi to Louisiana to our church was the highlight of the week. At five years old, the bridge seemed to be inordinately high. The old bridge was brown and looked like it would've collapsed at any moment.

Upon arriving at the old country church, we would be greeted by congregants and my closest little friends. The kids would dash off to the church basement, where we would entertain ourselves. Our favorite thing to do was mimic adult church service. We would sing songs from the hymnal. Each kid would take turns leading the bible verse reading, as the older kids would assist those of us who couldn't quite read. Then, someone would take up the collection. Our pennies and nickels would average about two dollars a week. By this time, the adult service was taking up their offering. We would proudly parade in a single line to the church service with our collection in our hands.

But my parents' work was beyond the four walls of the church. When God called my parents to Mississippi in the early '60s, He showed them visions of a greatly impoverished people in deplorable living conditions. We would frequently go to various homes, visiting families in need that had no way of getting to church. There was one particular route we would take during these home visits that always made me uneasy. I would cling to my mother's dress from the time we got out of the car, until the time we returned and headed back to the main road. We'd venture through the deep back woods, where we'd reach these decrepit cabins.

Situated on an old plantation, now in ruins, stood several rows of one-room slave quarters nearly a ½-mile or so away. Small and dilapidated, most cabins had decaying steps and doors hanging off the hinges. However, people lived here, and my parents were told these residents needed help. We would bring food and clothing, and often we would be invited inside these homes. As the "town reverend," Dad was well-known for his caring words of hope and encouragement. A young girl that particularly comes to my mind lived in one of these shabby cabins. When we would come to the door, her mother would open it and this girl, approximately seven or eight years old, would crawl nearby to investigate the commotion. As we walked into the home, the little girl would start grunting in fear, then scurry to the back of the cabin, hiding under a table. She would remain there for the duration of our visit. She never walked upright, but on all fours. I don't remember ever hearing her utter one word. This young girl paced back and forth under the table. The walls were covered with cockroaches, and a pot of urine and feces overflowed. I can remember, as a small child, seeing roaches on the baby's bottle and feeling sick. Even as a young child, it was obvious to me that this family was broken and hurting in every way: they needed to know Jesus.

Lately, when talking to my father about these visits, he was amazed I remembered the plantation. My recent prayer for that young girl, if she was still alive, is that she found a safe home. I believe the words my parents spoke in the cabin made a difference.

However, our home wasn't a reflection of our church life. Instead, it was chaotic, with intense agitation between my parents. Their inability to somehow handle their emotions would result in anger, screaming, overturned furniture and, on several occasions, physical altercations. On these shocking occasions, a sharp, clenching feeling would create a knot in my stomach right before my heart started fiercely pounding. I wanted to hide under my bed to escape the scary sounds that seemed to penetrate the walls of our house. If only our walls could talk, they would tell the truth that lay behind the perfect imagery of our fairytale family portrait they hung on our living room wall. These walls could reveal the hidden, gruesomely-recurrent indignation that plagued our war-zone home.

The dysfunctional relationship between my parents caused us to move away from the big beautiful white house on the hill. All my church friends, whom I had learned to call my family, were now a distant memory. Besides, it had only been a few years earlier that we had moved from my birth home.

Starting a fresh life in a new city was quite contrary to my familiar rural surroundings. My father no longer pastored a church, and my parents both worked to keep a roof over our heads. For many years, their relationship intensified toward a downward spiral, despite my mother giving birth to my two brothers. Mom had my brothers three years apart in age. Sadly, the joy of new baby arrivals in the house was short-lived before returning to the love-empty house.

During this time, the responsibilities of being a big sister were in full effect. Every morning, Mom would place a key around my neck. She would say, "Now, Lee Ann, keep this around your neck. This is the key to enter the apartment." Looking intense, as she lowered her head, she continued, "And if you lose it, you won't be able to get into the apartment." My chest would rise and fall with rapid breaths as I exhaled, anticipating the daily routine.

As a young child, I experienced daily anxiety attacks due to fearful ordeals I encountered alone. I felt overwhelmed taking the bus from school to our apartment building, riding the elevator to the fifth floor, and letting myself inside the apartment. The babysitter who was caring for my brothers would eventually come and get me. But, the waiting time for her to pick me up felt like an eternity. Therefore, to ease such fearful emotions, I would sneak into the refrigerator to find comfort. Eating had a strange way of making me feel a little safer. Food allowed me to slip away from the pain of the present to a place where responsibility for the future was in my hands. I would often get in trouble for sneaking food. My entire life began to revolve around food. Happiness became hinged on what I ate.

At night, I would have beautiful dreams of trees on my wall, growing bigger and bigger. Other times, I experienced nightmares of fire consuming everything I loved. My heart would be filled with fear, but there was no one safe to tell.

Unfortunately, during this time, the oldest of my brothers, who was three at the time, was diagnosed with multiple sclerosis and was told by my parents that he may never walk. From that day forward, it seemed that my parents' relationship was hinging on a single thread. The toll of my brother's illness and their already unhealthy relationship was no match for survival. Soon after, they were divorced.

My mom worked all day and into the evening. Being only eight years old, I was given the grave responsibility of caring for my brothers. There wasn't any opportunity to grieve over the divorce or a speed class on how to become an eight-year-old "little mommy." My grades suffered greatly: reports from school frequently said I lacked focus in class. But after school, I cooked, cleaned, and cared for my little brothers. Consequently, the doctors had been right; the oldest of my brothers, who is five years my junior, never walked. Inevitably, it became my job, and eventually my responsibility to carry him, feed him, and keep him happy. My youngest brother and I would keep him highly entertained with singing, laughing, and storytelling while Mom was away.

However, Mom would come home, resting her hands on her hips, complaining and saying, "You can't take care of your own home properly." Lifting my shoulder in a half-shrug was my only response. Being occupied with parental duties left no time to clean the house.

As we got older, we would take our brother outside in his wheelchair, when it wasn't broken and if the apartment elevator was working. But much of the time was spent indoors. I believed if I could keep my brothers laughing, they wouldn't feel the sadness and the fear of condemnation that my mom would make me feel. The chatter in my head grew louder, "What if you drop him while bathing him? He'll slip down into the water." At other times, I would hear, "He's going to choke on your cooking, and you won't be able to dislodge it." Thinking to myself, "I would go to jail and get the death penalty." So, in order to quiet the adolescent head chatter, we would just play more, eat more, laugh more, and write more songs.

During this time, I was becoming quite a cook and did lots of tasting. Besides, it calmed my nerves. The pounds continued to grow, and my habitual eating habits resulted in thick arms and flabby thighs.

I resolved no longer to spend time standing in front of the freezer scooping ice-cream from the carton with a finger. No more snacking over the stove, tasting from spaghetti sauces intended for the family dinner. Telling myself frequently, "It's a half cup of raw vegetables, one boiled egg, vitamins, and a grim (possibly slim), future."

Throughout my teen years, I had managed to keep my brothers alive. Thankfully, during this time, Mom could afford help in assisting with the boys. I began venturing into the world to create a life for myself. Being cocooned and extremely emotionally overwhelmed had contributed to the weight gain. Ultimately, my appearance became another source of condemnation. I began a dialogue with fat. "I hate the way you crinkle around my legs and the way you fold my stomach in three parts when I bend over." Fat responded, "But you've been hating me for quite a long time. I think it's time to consider something you have been overlooking: If you really wanted me to go away, I would be gone. You are the one who won't let me go. I have no investment in being here. All you have to do is want me to be gone and I will be." Regrettably, the weight continued to escalate to numerical proportions. Teen angst was in full bloom; I was overwhelmed by anxiety and wondering if everything was well at home when I was away. Nevertheless, I mustered up the nerve to venture out with girlfriends.

My relationship with God had always been my bedrock, as far as I could remember. The dreams I encountered were like streams of water to my thirsty soul. Countless times, I tried to convince myself I was dreaming, and that the euphoria I felt was some "happy brain chemical" I had accessed. But this was God's way of showing me His love toward me and the bright future He had in store for me. As I look back, God was preparing me for the turmoil that I soon encountered in life.

One night, while my best friend and I exited our neighborhood movie theater, a man in his car pulled up to us asking for directions. Simultaneously, I proceeded to a nearby payphone to call home and advise of our current status, while my friend walked over to the man's car engaging in conversation. This was her typical response, as she was much more comfortable with the opposite sex than I. After putting my hand in my pants pocket, I quickly discovered I only had a dollar bill and a quarter, but no dime for the phone call. Upon reaching the car, I was soon informed that this guy "Dave" was new to the area and had gotten "turned around" and lost.

It was our town's "Cruise Night" on the boulevard. Some of the streets were blocked off in order for the decked-out motorcycles and low-riders to show off their intricate paint jobs and hydraulics. Random detours would make it somewhat difficult to navigate the streets if one was unfamiliar with the neighborhood. We gave Dave directions, and the three of us ended up talking and watching the festivities together for a short time. He casually offered to drive us home, and by this time, we were feeling comfortable with him. Dave was well-groomed and a very polite young man. He didn't appear to be evil, nasty, nor a scruffy-looking dude who lurks in the bushes or shadows of a parking garage. So, we accepted the offer. Besides, we lived only a few miles down the highway. Sadly, Dave never took us home.

Dave cruised the boulevard for a while, assuring us that he would take us home shortly. We noticed an open case of beer in the back seat, of which he had been drinking and continued to drink while cruising. Dave's demeanor gradually started to change. My friend Lucille informed him that we really should have been home long ago. It was only a matter of time before our families would be looking for us. We both started asking Dave to let us out so we could notify our parents concerning our whereabouts. But it was to no avail; he stopped talking and ignored us. Dave became increasingly aggravated – angered by our requests. I tried a calmer, friendlier approach, assuring him that we would love to see him again and introduce him to other sights in our city. My attempts seemed to calm him down for a brief moment. Unfortunately, due to the large amount of alcohol consumed, Dave grew intensely unstable and violent.

As Lucille began demanding Dave to stop the vehicle, he stopped the car long enough to push her into the back seat and assault her. It was a vicious, brutal attack. As I glanced in the back seat, I witnessed twisted arms, pinning, dominance, and a taunting scene. It was as if a little voice in his mind was telling him it's alright to crave the kind of pain and emotional abuse he inflicted.

Dave transformed into a monster. In his mind, he was a predator determined to attack, and we were his prey. His eyes were bloodshot and cloudy, empty and frozen. His eyes made me want to run. He glared at me like he was hunting me down. His face was lifeless as he drove away from the city and into a deserted region that I didn't even know existed. Dave seemed to be familiar with this route. It was useless begging and pleading for Dave to release us. Instinctively, our cries only angered him to yell. Foul language was bouncing off the interior of the car. Dave continued swinging his arms and striking us, while dangerously speeding down dark, long streets.

We eventually came to rest in a place with no streetlights or paved roads; it was pitch black. The ill-lighted surroundings were caving in around us. Dave got out of the car, went to his trunk, and returned with a gun, making lots of threats if we didn't take him seriously. This monster slammed my head on the seat of the car so hard I thought I would lose consciousness. I bound my hands tight around my pants so he wouldn't take them off. Nevertheless, Dave yanked my hands away. He squeezed them tightly, while gazing into my eyes. I couldn't stop crying as he roughly pulled down my pants and underwear.

The subsequent hours were horrifying. We were abused and beaten over and over again. It was humiliating, vile, and torturous. By closing my eyes, my mind had managed to escape for a few minutes trying to silence the haunting ordeal. I was terrified. Gruesome thoughts were filling my head. I kept trying to mentally escape. My mind wanted to go to a "happy place." I tried everything to get my mind off this terribly dehumanizing ordeal. At various times, I lost all awareness of me, turning into several different personas. Each personality was trying to stay alive by any means necessary! Since pretending was a thing I had learned to do well, I tried to befriend Dave in between the times I kicked and punched. When I no longer believed we would be rescued, and were moments from being killed, I gave myself permission to "lose it." I started screaming as loud as I could for as long as possible, despite his blows and threats. My resolve was to unconsciously go within myself to another place. Once there, I figured out a master plan that assured I would survive. An instant calm fell over me.

Once Dave was done tormenting us and raised his gun to shoot, I planned to do something truly fantastic. Immediately after I heard him cock his gun and shoot, I plotted to speedily turn my body to the side. In this way, I'd let the bullet hit me in the arm. Then, I would quickly turn back, grab my chest and fall to the ground, appearing to be dead. I would lay there until Dave drove off. I would spring into action, running to get help for Lucille and myself. If my plan succeeded, we would be alive and safe. My mind became wonderfully at ease. I even sighed a relief, as my stomach was no longer in knots, for I had solved this awful plight and freedom was just moments away.

Inevitably, it wasn't until weeks later I realized I could never be faster than a speeding bullet. Nonetheless, in that place of dark and dismal isolation and during that time of overwhelming fear and hopelessness, peace had arrived.

When Dave decided he was finished, he calmed down and began talking to us semi-sanely again. We followed suit. Lucille and I told Dave we were fine, and it was the effect of the beer on him that caused this situation. We promised not to tell anyone what happened. It took a great deal of convincing Dave that all was forgiven. Eventually, he got in his car and drove off. A silenced passed. All we could hear was our own heavy breathing. After looking around, we didn't know where we were or in which direction to proceed. So, we just started walking. The ground was sandy and composed of small hill formations. It was difficult to maintain our footing. But, we kept a steady pace and pressed forward, accompanied only by darkness and fog.

Suddenly, deep down the highway, we spotted car lights. We were finally getting rescued – or so we thought. Sadly, we quickly discovered it was Dave's car heading toward us, thinking out loud, "He must have second thoughts and is back to finish the job."

Rows of trees bordered the highway, so we dashed into the thickness of the trees. Full branches were hanging low to the ground. It was clear we could hang on the tree trunks and not be seen. After a few minutes, we heard Dave get back into his car and drive away. We dared not move. Several more minutes passed before we slowly emerged, realizing Dave had gone. Once again, we escaped the jaws of death.

Time had escaped us as we walked before reaching the highway. We hiked along the shoulder of the highway, looking for a well-lit exit. All of a sudden, headlights were coming towards us on the highway. I knew it was Dave again. He must've decided to wait until we emerged from the dense trees. As the car approached us, I immediately began screaming and threw myself into the ditch on the side of the road. I didn't want to be seen. Ironically, Lucille became uncharacteristically calm, cool, and compassionate while remaining with me. Her constant reassurance that we were going to survive together brought a sense of ease. With every passing car, she held on to me, comforting and promising me that it wasn't Dave. We were exhausted. It had been at least six to eight hours of this hideous ordeal. With the passing of each car, I screamed, ran hysterically, stiffened, and lost all self-control. It must have been hours before we made it to an all-night truck stop and asked someone to contact the police.

We were taken immediately to the hospital for examinations and provided a detailed report to the officers and detectives assigned to our case. The reunion with my mom was very emotional for both of us. As we locked eyes, a sense of anguish transferred between us. But, the mere realization that I lived to see her was shocking.

Dave was arrested that next morning. I later learned the reason he had come back after leaving us wasn't because he planned on killing us. He lost his wallet in the sand. However, he wasn't able to locate it. So, he left the scene and went home to his wife and children.

The police found the location we had described, along with tire tracks leading to the scene of the assault. They found Dave's wallet with his driver's license, which led to his home address.

Weeks before the trial, feelings of helplessness surrounded me like an invisible cloak.

On the morning of the trial, I could hardly breathe; the thought of seeing Dave again sickened me. I located a plastic tumbler from the kitchen and filled it with orange juice, leaving room for some of my mom's gin hidden under the sink. I managed to swallow the awful taste before entering the car and heading over to the courthouse. Unbeknownst to me, this drink would be a "go-to" for comfort – other than food. In the years that followed, I would rely on a mixed drink for the relief of sadness, loneliness, and anxiety.

Dave's verdict returned quickly, and he was convicted. But this whole ordeal wasn't by any means over. It was a long time before images of the ordeal ceased to invade my thoughts on a daily basis. He was a gang member, and due to threats from his "boys," we had to relocate again. This time, I was glad to move, but the residue of the abduction would live forever.

Over the years, if I talked about the abduction, it was in a monologue or play I had written. I played the part of myself, the victim, yet I didn't allow myself to experience true feelings other than those I felt for the poor girl I was portraying. Inwardly, I distanced myself from emotions. Once, in a speech tournament, I shared the tragedy about a young girl's abduction and her struggle through fear and brokenness, but justice prevailed. I gave the speech several times in various levels of the tournament and was hailed as quite the young writer, taking home a shiny trophy. The speech was entitled "My First Kiss."

I couldn't talk to counselors about the abduction or any of my inner feelings. The impregnable constant nagging was an inner voice that wouldn't be quiet. Besides, how would I begin to work on myself, focus on my issues, and love myself through this inconceivable pain? One of the most remarkable features of the human mind is our incredible capacity to forget, ignore, or in other ways avoid things that trouble us. This devastating traumatic experience paralyzed me in a web of conflicting emotions, thereby creating a void. I felt a loss of faith in my personal safety, order, and continuity in my life. I was reexperiencing distress and emotional numbness.

Depression started to grip me as it gained momentum. Its plan was to steal my joy, destroy my future, and end my life. I was diagnosed with clinical depression.

My love for cooking drove me to chef's school while continuing writing, acting, and singing. During this time, I had a small production company and toured with some of my musical productions. Up to that point, this was the happiest I had ever been. My life was happy, while acting.

Unaware of dating, the inability to choose the right man landed me in an unhealthy relationship. Looking for love, without knowing how to choose wisely, led me into marriage within a short period of time after meeting this man. The marriage was short-lived, but through the union my son "Luke" was born. He was gorgeous. Growing up, Luke had become my best friend and greatest fan. Luke loved my storytelling. He'd say, "Mommy, tell me a story without a book." He would listen with the widest of eyes as I included him in an African Bush adventure. Other than my beautiful son, I felt my life was so far removed from knowing who I was and why I existed. I began to cry out and call on Jesus. If He was real, and not just the figment of a lonely little girl's imagination, He was there to find and help me. Well, after frantically calling on God for several weeks, He answered. We ended up at a church where I rededicated my life to Him, and I remain a member of that church to this day.

In my Christian growth, there came a time where He began teaching me to trust Him. I learned how God was able to keep, provide, and protect me. As I began to take these new steps in God's Kingdom, I was astounded that pain was unearthed within me. It was as if my foundation was crumbling. Little did I realize it was so filled with sand. Fear, anxiety, and depression was short-circuiting my fuel for life. Electing to drop out of society, preferring my room with the lights off and the curtains drawn became my place of refuge. I began sleeping more throughout the day, hastily returning home from my errands to return to my place of safety within the dark cave. Doctors were content with prescribing me various medications as a bandage for temporary relief. But even with pills, I still had to care for my son, manage my affairs, interact with people, and appear "somewhat normal."

I had managed sadness all my life, but something was different. A beast was emerging, rising up with dark solutions to my plight.

The emotional pain was increasing, tiredness was wearing me like a badge of honor. I was immensely medicated, so overcome with responsibilities that I could no longer pretend I knew how to handle life. Without any strength to seek God, I couldn't find my place of peace. Darkness was aggressively seeking me out. His voice was familiar; I remember hearing from him in previous hard times. He didn't present himself as mean or harsh, but more as an old friend who wanted to get reacquainted with me again. I remember he used to whisper to me as a child when I heard Mom and Dad fight. Darkness visited me after the abduction— keeping me company, as I stared up from my bed, unable to talk or interact with anyone. As I listened to him, his faint voice was growing louder, sounding like a concerned friend with all the answers. He spoke from inside my head, and unlike anyone else, he understood why sleep had been the best answer thus far. Darkness began to convince me that ultimate relief would come if I slept and never had to wake up again.

He devised a plan for me. I would insert a problem with the plan, "But what about my son, or what if the pills don't work?" Darkness had all the answers. The more I entertained his familiar voice, the more anticipation grew for obtaining relief. I drove myself to a secluded place to bring closure to a life I could no longer tolerate. I hoarded my pills, brought a knife along as a backup, and lit a fire in my car, putting into action the plan that we had worked out over the past months. But God intervened; it wasn't time for me to go. I fell asleep before I could ingest all the pills. Someone saw the flames and called the authorities. I was in restraints before I could carry out another step of the plan. God had another plan, and the suicide attempt was unsuccessful. Today, life expectancy is higher than it's ever been, but the suicide rate is on the rise - perhaps indicating that our country's mental-health management is lagging behind the rest of medicine.

Confused and muddied, I found myself in the hospital for weeks of treatment. It would be a long, hard-fought battle. The belief that I was no longer deserving of God's love seemed real. But He guaranteed that I would make it. God began a process of uprooting a lifetime of foul and unstable foundations.

Deliverance came in so many wonderful waves of time spent with my Savior. Praying and worshipping Him, continually in His presence became my backdrop of security. I learned to love Him in a new and fresh way.

One day while studying Genesis, one of my favorite books in the Bible, an awareness of the sweet, loving connection He had with Adam in the garden began to become my reality. It was then that He showed me a garden of trees. He said that I was destined to dwell with Him forever. I would be a witness, a Tree of Righteousness for all men to see and witness His abiding love for humanity.

God spoke to my heart and said when the enemy abducted me and sought to kill me, He was there. Just as He moved through the trees in the garden with Adam, He was with me in the orange grove, moving through the trees to keep me alive. It was His spirit that gave me the strength to fight. It was Him that caused the wallet to fall on the ground and the tracks of Dave's tires to be set in the sand, providing clear-cut evidence that justice would be served.

My Lord knows the encroachments and the strongholds that you would have to contend with, but have no condemnation. He is not the author of trouble, but He will walk us out of it if we stay with Him through the fire. Let the outcome of your trials be GOOD, gaining TRUST in GOD as He makes manifest the miraculous works of His hands in your life.

When you can't fix it, humble yourself and cry out for your Savior! Run to the light! Diligently seek your Lord, and don't stop until you've gained entrance into the secret place.

Then... REST there, LISTEN there. Let Him love you there. Your roots will GROW there.

I now SEE Victory AHead

Bruised, But Not Broken...

Self-Reflection
Chapter 1

1. What keeps you from telling your story?

   Embarrassment   Fear of Rejection

   Shame   Guilt

   Exhaustion   Pride

2. What is the hardest thing to accept about your story? Why?

3. How can you use your story to serve or help others in dark places?

Chapter 2

BREAKING THE CYCLE

During my mom's pregnancy with me, she was serving time in prison. To this day, she's never been able to overcome addiction and remain drug-free. Sadly, I can't imagine the extremely stressful experience of being pregnant in jail. Besides, there is an incredible high level of uncertainty when it comes to giving birth while incarcerated. Inmates and their families are rarely informed of the likely scheduled due date. These restrictions are in place to prevent women from getting outside help to plan escapes.

Seemingly mundane things, like providing urine samples, were done under the careful watch of an armed guard. Despite guards watching my mom around the clock, she still felt isolated. "It was a lonely time," my mom informed me.

After giving birth to me at Riverside County Hospital, Mom spent 24-hours with me before I was taken away. Our family was kept in the dark regarding my birth details. They learned about my delivery after Mom returned to prison. She returned to prison a few days after my birth. My grandparents were given custody of me, however,

Mom told my grandparents not to get financial support for me. Mom wanted to ensure she could receive financial assistance once released from prison.

Immediately after being released, Mom started abusing drugs again. Crack cocaine was her "drug of choice." Shortly after Mom's release, she moved my four siblings and me to my Auntie Ree's place. We lived there with my aunt and her children. Nevertheless, Mom spiraled into a drug-infused lifestyle. Daily, my adolescent life was unpredictable. Days wavered between Mom refusing to get out of bed in the morning to times when my four sisters and I were left to fend for ourselves.

The saddening byproduct of Mom's neglect convinced my Uncle Roy to contact the Department of Children and Family Services (DCFS). We were taken away by the police. Being taken away from Mom and Auntie's house was the first trauma I experienced. I thought I was being placed into foster care because I was naughty. But shortly thereafter, I learned I was placed into foster care because Mom wasn't a good parent.

On that night, torrential rain hit the windshield of the car. I thought that windshield would break at any second. I crunched my teeth over my lip. Salty blood filled my mouth. The paralyzing feeling spread throughout my body like icy, liquid metal. I felt frozen in one place, wide-eyed, with trembling hands and shallow breathing.

While sitting in the back seat of the squad car, sounds of sirens and lights flashing gripped our hearts. Rotating sweeps of light were bright and glittery. I held my breath with eyes fixed unnaturally ahead. As my sisters grasped each other's hands, my stomach and throat were throbbing in balls of knots. Assuming the officer wanted to ease the pain from our shattered hearts and confused minds, he asked, "Do you guys want ice cream?" Without hesitation, we nodded our heads – too afraid to utter a word.

We drove up to McDonald's to get ice cream, which apparently eased the fear. Watching cars on the street was our escape. My sisters and I played the game of counting all the cars we passed. Finally reaching our destination, we arrived at a house in Pasadena. Prior to exiting the car, one of the policemen said, "This will be your home for a few weeks." My sisters and I began smiling. We were looking forward to returning to Auntie Ree's house. But, immediately flowing from his lips was the crushing comment, "Until we can find you a permanent place to live." Observing the disappointment etched on our face, the policeman uttered, "This is a nice house and you will all be well taken care of." Bewildered and uncertain of the policeman's thoughts, we shrugged our shoulders.

Upon entering the house, we were greeted by a lady whose thin, dark face appeared somewhat weathered. She had a mixture of gray and black hair that was wiry in texture. Her smile was warm and inviting. She welcomed us inside as we said our goodbyes to the police officers.

"Hello, girls. Welcome to our home," she said in a soft tone.

The woman walked us around the house, introducing us to her husband, whom she called Mr. Roberts. With a pleasant demeanor, he shook our hands saying, "Hello, girls, so good to meet you." We replied, "Hello." Mr. Roberts asked, "Tell me your names. So, all five of you are sisters?" We nodded, "Yes." Mrs. Roberts swiftly prepared dinner for us. We ate dinner together on the dining room table. That night, there were no mayonnaise and bologna sandwiches or Kool-Aid served. Instead, we had a home-style meal served on plates.

It was a simple yet sensational array of seasoned and sizzling foods. We had never seen the variety of assorted colored vegetables displayed so beautifully. The next morning was Saturday, and we were awakened for breakfast. "Girls, it's time to awake. Breakfast is ready," Mrs. Roberts said in a smooth motherly tone.

My sisters and I were looking for sugary cereals. Instead, we were served eggs, bacon, pancakes, and milk. These were the biggest pancakes we had ever fastened our eyes on. We ate pancakes in the past, but they were frozen ones that you heat in the microwave. Our tummies were full and totally satisfied, to say the least.

After breakfast, Mrs. Roberts laid some clothes out for us to wear. She had been a foster parent for many years and frequently provided emergency shelter. Therefore, Mrs. Roberts had extra clothes for us. Many kids passed this way prior to being assigned a permanent home.

"Girls, we are going shopping today for new clothes. Tomorrow is Sunday, and you guys need Sunday clothes for church," she said. Mrs. Roberts smiled and hurried us to put on clothes and wash our hands. The five of us were sitting on the couch staring at the huge screen in front us while eagerly waiting to leave. We had never seen such a large television. It was encased in an elegant, huge, wooden entertainment console. Almost in unison, we shouted, "Wow!" We were mesmerized by the largeness of the TV and never noticed the cartoons playing on the screen.

By this time, Mrs. Roberts entered the living room, sitting down on a chair near the couch. "Well, girls, before we go shopping for clothes, let's have a little chat." She smiled as she continued. "Do you understand why you are here?" We looked at each other, checking to see who'd answer the question. Lilly, the eldest of us, replied, "The police told us we would be taken better care of here."

With streams of tears beginning to well up in her eyes, Mrs. Roberts replied, "Yes. That is the reason you are here, girls." Wiping tears from her eyes and looking at each one of us, she continued, "Hopefully, you will be away from your mom for a short period of time until she gets better." Not knowing what Mrs. Roberts meant, Lilly asked, "Our mom is sick?"

"Uh-huh. Something like that. But for now, you will be with me for a couple of weeks 'til we can find you all a place to stay for a longer time."

Mrs. Roberts gathered us together in the car, and we drove to Walmart to purchase clothes. She allowed us to pick out Sunday clothes for church. She told us, "Now, girls, pick something really nice. You have to look pretty for service tomorrow." However, we hadn't a clue what church was; we had never stepped foot in a church. Nevertheless, we were excited. Sunday morning couldn't get here soon enough.

Historically, Sunday morning worship service is the guaranteed place where African Americans went to "be somebody." Other days of the week, they struggled to achieve validation as "somebody," constantly fighting treatment as invisible and/or a misnomer. But, Sunday was different. The church seemed like a sanctuary. Grandparents, mothers, fathers, uncles, aunts, and all their children put on their "Sunday meeting" clothes and headed to church. Women wore wide-brimmed hats and long flowing dresses. Men wore crisp, white shirts and ties. Children smelled of perfumes added to their Saturday night bath water.

Sunday morning gave people a level of dignity they couldn't find on any other day of the week. Monday through Friday, women and men may have worked jobs as janitors or maids, nobly and respectably, but oftentimes, experiencing the indignity of being called "boy" or "girl," "auntie" or "uncle." Everybody needed his or her dose of "Precious Lord, Take My Hand." Here, parishioners could shout and sing and have their soul prepared for Monday through Friday. Mrs. Roberts called it, "Putting on God's body armor."

The choir would be singing, and drums would be beating as loudly as possible. Congregants would scream and shout while breathing heavy and hard into their faux microphones. Black women kept the church going. They were often relegated to the periphery of the church, yet remained integral to sustaining it. Women often participated in fundraising to help build and sustain the church.

One month after living with the Roberts, my sisters and I were introduced to Mrs. Edwards. She attended the same church. We met after service one Sunday while sitting on a church pew, ready to leave. As usual, it had been a lengthy service, and our stomachs were growling from hunger pangs.

"Girls, I would like you to meet Mrs. Edwards. She is a nice lady, and you will be moving in with her and her husband on Monday." Mrs. Roberts went on to say, "We will need to split the five of you up." Tearfully continuing, "Robin, you and Ebony will go and live with Mrs. Edwards. The other three of you girls will stay with me for a couple of weeks until a home opens up for you."

Emotionally scarred by the news, we looked down and echoed the word, "OK." While in emergency placement at the Roberts' home, I had learned we were in a safe place. I didn't want to leave the security we found. However, we had no choice.

So, we packed up our meager possessions and hugged Mrs. Roberts goodbye. We had no idea our lives would forever change. On the drive to our new home, I remember not wanting the drive to end. Countless thoughts were racing through my mind as we approached our new home. Ironically, it never crossed our minds we would never return to live with our Mom again.

The Edwards were our permanent family. This was our new home. My sister and I realized we were walking into this situation blindly. We didn't know how the Edwards lived nor how they did things. My sisters and I felt extremely uninformed about the whole process from DCFS. As an 8-year-old, this was a lot to mentally comprehend. The early years were pleasant yet awkward at the same time.

We settled into a small school. Everyone knew we were foster kids, and that was a stigma I had to overcome both in school and in the community. It was hard trying to adjust to a new school, fitting in, and dealing with your emotions all at the same time.

Eventually, the physical abuse started. Vividly, I remember getting beaten with extension cords, paddles, belts, and whatever else was at arm's length for her to reach. All of this was due to my room not being kept clean. On one occasion, I abruptly awoke from a deep sleep being beaten with an extension cord to my whole body. Mrs. Edwards then emptied the drawers. She angrily pulled everything out of the closet and said, "You and your sister haven't cleaned the room." This was about 1:00 a.m., and we didn't finish cleaning the room until 3:00 a.m. To top it off, we still had to get up for school that very morning.

Beatings became frequent. My foster mom would often say, "You girls have a bad attitude." I remember one year, my sister and I got beaten so badly with an extension cord that we had welts all over our bodies. Our backs were bleeding, and our foster mom poured alcohol on our backs, saying, "You shouldn't have been so bad."

Getting teased at school for having to wear Goodwill clothes and Payless shoes to school was totally embarrassing. As a strong-willed child, living on punishment became a way of life. While my younger sister and friends were allowed to watch movies, I was stuck in my room on punishment.

Many of my birthdays were never celebrated, and feeling like I was only tolerated brought on more bitterness.

The emotional pain that I was experiencing and feelings of abandonment were growing with each passing day. The uncertainty of my future appeared dim. My eyes were broken faucets. I would get easily irritated and cry often. Sometimes, I felt my heart was being crushed. I constantly heard Mrs. Edwards' voice in my mind. It was an endless cycle of criticism with her saying, "You should have done this. You should not have done that. You could've done..."

My thoughts drew me deeper and deeper into a black hole. I felt like I was suffocating. My life was caving in on me.

Abandonment issues stemmed from my childhood loss. It caused significant impairment, particularly with regard to the development of healthy relationships. Consequently, I was likely to encounter long-term psychological challenges based on a fear that abandonment would reoccur. It had become evident that I lacked self-esteem as a result of childhood abandonment. These issues also led to a continual struggle with mood swings and anger throughout my life.

Finally, for the first time, my foster mom took Robin and me to L.A. We went to visit my natural family. This was the time the anger that I was feeling began to surface. We saw our grandparents, sisters, and mom. My mom was still in her addiction, which angered me even more to witness. She was slumped in a lounge chair. My mother's state veered dramatically, seemingly every minute.

She sat there that afternoon discussing her drug abuse. She disavowed the crack addict she was as though it were a separate spirit that had taken over her body. Mom even said that she had chased "it" out solely through the brute strength of her own newly-discovered willpower. After acknowledging her addiction and redemption in the same breath, she went on to offer a laundry list of reasons why my sister and I should never do drugs.

My mother went on to let us know that she had "done it all"– PCP, LSD, an assortment of pills, both "uppers" and "downers," often mixed up together in an assortment of self-administered cocktails of her own creation.

All of my expectations of a grand reunion with my family were quickly dissolved, and we were on our way back home.

It seemed like I had become her enemy, and there was no reprieve from the harsh and abusive treatment from my foster mother.

She once yanked me out of bed so hard by my legs that I slammed down to the floor with a force that knocked the air out of my chest. I would then follow her into the kitchen while she banged the kitchen cabinets. "I suppose you want breakfast," she'd snap, while I stood still, my hands balled into tiny fists by my sides.

So, I'd give a stiff little nod, and in response, she'd grab a plastic bowl from a shelf and hurl it in my general direction. After ducking out of the way, I'd pick up the bowl from the floor and proceed to the refrigerator for milk. My silence enraged her more, so did my tears. Frequently, I opted for silence in hope of being as inconspicuous as possible. Often, she'd grab me by my hair or neck, pulling me back toward her as I walked past.

"When I was your age, I could scramble eggs, but you can only pour yourself cereal. You're useless," she said as she let go of me.

Another of my failures was an inability to properly braid my hair, which my foster mother would gripe about as she attacked my scalp with the plastic teeth of her comb. On the occasions when I squirmed too much or she was confronted with an especially stubborn knot, she would drag me across the peeling particleboard floor by my mane. Simultaneously, she wildly waved a pair of scissors in the other hand threatening to take away the only part of me I knew to be pretty. I'd stand there sobbing, my fingers shakily trying to thread three thick strands together while her scissors pointed tauntingly at my head. Eventually, she'd give up on the threat and settle for a hit across my head.

Somehow, the news of the abuse had gotten to DCFS, and they had scheduled a home visit. It was made clear by our foster mother that she wasn't going to lose her license, and we were instructed to deny any allegations of physical child abuse.

Ms. Arnold, the social worker, arrived the next day with her business card and a notepad in her hand. By the look on her face, it was as if she was on a mission. She was there to investigate the complaint. Her focus was on ensuring the social, physical, psychological, and emotional well-being of her clients. Her goal was to protect children from situations of abuse, neglect, and other forms of maltreatment.

Upon her arrival, she asked my foster mom, "Is there anywhere I can speak to the girls privately?"

"Sure," she replied, "As a matter of fact, you can use the girls' room."

Once we entered the room, Ms. Arnold began to ask us a series of questions. We answered all the questions, keeping in mind if we told the truth we would possibly be abused even more by our foster mom.

Being afraid of the ramifications that could possibly surface, we denied any abuse.

From that time on she ceased with all noticeable physical abuse, but instead would make us write standards and or stand against the wall with our foot held up, not touching the ground, with an encyclopedia placed on our heads. At other times, we were taken to the church altar and forced to kneel for long periods. Mrs. Edwards called me and my sister bad kids and would say, "Ask God for forgiveness."

At ten years old, I was allowed to join a girls' basketball team. During practice, Amber, a girl on my team, jammed into my arm. The grueling pain began traveling through my whole arm. After arriving home in severe pain and in tears, my foster mom wouldn't take me to the doctor. She replied, "There is nothing wrong with you. You're faking." Finally, after three days, my foster dad took me to the emergency room, and it was confirmed that I had fractured my arm. A cast was placed on it. Upon arriving home with the cast on my arm, she still insisted that I didn't need the cast and that I was faking the injury.

During these years, my depression and feeling miserable continued.

At age 14, I remember one particular night like it was yesterday. I was sharing a room with my foster sister, Jocelyn. Abruptly waking up gasping for air during the night, Jocelyn was on top of me with her fist around my throat. There was no time for tears of screams, just sheer reaction. I immediately threw up my forearms like an offensive lineman blocking a defensive back. Jocelyn tried to slip to the side, pushing my elbow down and away. I slipped to the left, which threw her off and I landed on top. I slapped her with my open left hand full across the face. I deeply exhaled and inhaled again. My head swam and my stomach tightened.

Robin, my baby sister, leaped out of the next bed screaming, "Stop it!" I was feeling too exhausted to respond; all I could utter was a sigh. Robin had witnessed the entire ordeal and ran to inform my foster mom while I continued restraining Jocelyn.

"What in the world is going on here?" she shouted while entering the bedroom.

I immediately responded back, "She tried to choke me out!" Mrs. Edwards literally didn't believe my side of the story and went on a rampage that it was my fault.

Unbeknownst to me, the police were called, and I informed them to take me away from this house or else I was going to run away. So, they agreed to take me to an emergency shelter. From there I was moved to a level 4 group home. I transferred to Heritage Group Home in Whittier, California. While there, I was introduced to the drug crystal methamphetamine. Its effect was unpredictable, causing rapid mood swings, prominent delusions, and violent behavior.

I was looking to fit in and be accepted. Many of the girls were older than me, so I was often bullied.

Many people falsely think that bullying others as well as getting bullied by others is a part of everyone's life. Contrary to this misbelief, the truth is that bullying affected me beyond my imagination. The effect of bullying stayed with me for a long time–possibly my entire lifetime.

Needless to say, I experienced depression on various different levels. The feeling of being insulted is not easy to handle, especially when you are dealing with kids. Loneliness and sadness engulfed me.

Joining the Whittier High School basketball team was my way of escape from the life that was handed to me. I was finding ways to cope with my mom's decision of choosing drugs over her children. However, the one thing I was good at was short-lived; I got involved in a fight with two girls on the team.

During the next few years, I was moved to four group homes, juvenile hall, and spent a few months in jail due to fighting and non-compliance. During this time, I enlisted in Job Corps and met my son's father. Once we were released from Job Corps, we moved in with his parents. Unfortunately, at this place drama was staring me in the face. Again, I had entered a volatile relationship.

One night, as an issue started with my boyfriend's father and mother, it escalated to extreme violence. My boyfriend's father pushed me while I was holding my son in my arms. I ended up falling back, unable to protect him. My son hit his head on the Xbox console that was next to the television. Before I knew it, I had grabbed a knife and attempted to stab my boyfriend's father. Moments later, I found myself and my son standing outside in the cold. My son was screaming at the top of his lungs.

Fortunately, there was a police car near the house, and they drove me to the hospital. My son was diagnosed with a slight fracture in his head. While there, Child Protective Services came into the hospital room and took my son. How could this be happening? I started having flashbacks of when my sisters and I were taken from my mom. Now, it was 21 years later. Feelings of abandonment were filling me like poisonous venom flowing through my body. Feelings of being demoralized and dehumanized were gripping every thought.

Child Protective Services wouldn't give my son to his paternal grandmother, due to her record with the law. Therefore, he was placed in a foster home. During this time, I was living with one of my sisters. Eventually, I asked my sister to take custody of him, and she agreed. But because my son was under court guardianship, I was no longer allowed to remain in the house. Once again, I was in a tumultuous position with no place to live. Fortunately, I had a high school friend who lived in close proximity to my sister's house. She allowed me to rent a room. But once again, a physical altercation occurred between me and my friend. Furious feelings of anger escalated. It was like a light switch. All you needed was to push that wrong button, and something sent electricity down my spine, like unwanted energy.

I was raging, feeling trapped in a cage, trying to escape with my fists. Lashing blindly and all my reason had gone out of the window. Here we were in the kitchen, she had thrown a baby stroller at me and was now headed for a broom. I lunged forward to push her, and she flew into the stove where beans were cooking. I was running as fast as I could to my sister's house. My chest was heaving, and my shirt was billowing. The sound of my shoes hitting the pavement was loud. I jumped over a hedge and onto the pavement, then gasped for air. I had escaped to my sister's house where my son was living. In exhaustion, I ran through the front door, sounding off as fast as I could, relaying to my sister what had happened.

Within days, while sitting holding my son on the couch, police vehicles pulled up to the residence. They forced themselves into the house saying, "There is a warrant for your arrest." They took my son out of my hands, placing handcuffs on me. While stating my Miranda rights, the police officers simultaneously informed me that a victim had filed an assault charge. The victim stated I had picked up a steal metal hot pan with my hands and threw it at her.

Driving away in the police car brought back memories of me sitting in the police car as a little girl. Once again, I felt alone, helpless, powerless, wholly unable to act, and imprisoned in a cage. I was booked and charged with assault with a deadly weapon and placed in a holding cell. Hours later, a woman officer entered my cell, where other women were being held.

The officer said, "I need you to strip down. Take off all your clothes. Let your hair down, and raise your breasts." In an even louder tone, she gave more commands. "Put your feet apart. Turn around and bend over." The next instructions were to spread my vagina and cough hard. Afterward, we were instructed to put on the jail clothes provided for us. We were then placed in a freezing cold jail cell.

This would be my home for seven months while fighting a life sentence!

Consequently, I found a new lifeline. Being placed in the school dorm, working a good program, and having bible study with the chaplains gave me a new sense of hope. Eventually, the time had arrived for a few of our cases to be heard by the judge. Jared, the chaplain, gave me a prayer for daily meditation. It is found in Ephesians 6:10. Chaplain Jared instructed me to pray this every day and night, in the holding tank, and before entering the courtroom.

Well, on the day of my last offer before trial, I remember reciting the prayer exactly how Chaplain Jared told me. My public defender, Mrs. Ralph, entered the holding tank. "Ms. Hawkins, my advice to you is for you to take the eight years that they are offering you. Sitting there seemed like an eternity, wondering how I was going to be away from my son for eight whole years. I wondered who would take care of him.

Mrs. Ralph again entered back into the holding tank. Looking intense and confused, she said, "I don't know how it happened, but you must have God on your side." Releasing a sigh of relief, "The D.A. is offering you four years and possibly doing only 85% of the four years, and will change the charges to mayhem." Looking at the wall, she proceeded, "I know it's a lot, but you should take it." At this time, nervous and pacing the floor, she then stated in a firm tone, "If you go to trial and lose, it is a life sentence."

Listening to all the details, I felt in my heart to take the deal. Returning to jail I was indeed sad, but I was relieved I would see my son again. I was sentenced to Chowchilla State Prison. What's the worst thing about being moved to a prison? Probably the lottery you face on arrival. I asked myself the questions, "What's my new cellmate going to be like? Will she be a serial killer or an unpredictable psychopath? Or, will she be some poor woman suffering from some kind of mental illness who really should be in a hospital?

After a long journey in the prison transport, I was herded into a new wing and stopped on the landing outside the door of my new lodgings. Upon completing the intake process, I was given my blue-and-white, polka-dot prison attire and was placed temporarily for three- to four-weeks in a cell with one other person. I was there until they moved me to a seven-unit cell.

The banging, noises, smells, and emotions are a constant reminder that your life is no longer yours. You'll be eating your dinner in your cell while your cellmate is on the toilet next to you.

Everything becomes unbearable. The psychological punishment was the worst. You'd go into a cell, and everything would be just so—shoes lined up against the wall—people develop OCD. Inmates did all they could to control their environment. The huge fear of violence was everywhere. Violence and extreme violence were happening daily. Alarm bells were constantly ringing. I hadn't a clue whom to trust. You ask yourself, "Why are they talking to me? What do they want from me?"

The environment was caving in on me, and I requested to be transferred closer south to my family. Unfortunately, I was required to do two years before being allowed to be transferred. By God's grace, I made it through by only participating in one fight. Once, after being transferred, disappointment and frustration began to escalate. My family members wouldn't bring my son to visit me. And, again, my anger started to surface. My defiance to the guards became insurmountable, therefore, I was confined to my quarters and monitored by a staff member.

On one particular night, I needed to take my psych medication as a result of PTSD, due to the prison transition. The guard refused to give me medication, so I acted out in a violent rage. Afterward, she handcuffed me then pepper sprayed me over my entire body. This resulted in a bad asthma attack. I couldn't breathe. In the aftermath, I was placed in solitary confinement. This small solitary confinement and chains only allowed me to walk a few feet within the cell, and I was fed through a small hole.

Regrettably, the officer filed false charges against me, which said I committed battery on a staff member. Sadly, I remained in solitary confinement for seven months. The isolation of solitary confinement provides an escape from the yelling and chaos of the general inmate population and is almost a relief—for about the first 20 minutes. Then, you realize that the horror film cliché, "No one can hear you scream," has come true.

The staff thought it was funny to push the white, take-out style boxes that my meals came in off the tray slot before I could catch them, causing food to spill on the floor. My solitary confinement cell didn't get cleaned regularly or completely. Tumbleweeds of female hair - mine and others' - scattered around the floor and mixed with the food. As trays were dumped over two weeks, the residue of meals would build up. The only way I could clean the mess was to scoop the food up and flush it, while my toilet still worked. I had one towel for my thrice-weekly showers and scant toilet paper. I wasn't going to waste them wiping up liquid shepherd's pie.

When the meal was two bags of cornflakes and an apple, there was nothing to spill, so they just tossed the brown bag hard enough to bruise the fruit. In an abject display of my hunger, I rushed to pick up the bag. Solitary shrinks a person with helplessness. And I did shrink. One time, when the commanding officer tossed the tray filled with chicken à la king's gelatinous gravy across the floor, leaving withered peas, red peppers, and carrot cubes in a milky trail where it slid, I ate about three vegetables from the muck and then was mortified by behavior that no one else would ever see.

Prison infantilized me inside, but inmates in the general population have brief romances with resourcefulness as they roam the facility. They can walk to the staff's desk and ask for toilet paper. They can mail a letter. They can march up to a lieutenant in the dining hall and ask for help with an obstinate guard. Not so in solitary. Theoretically, you can report a problem to a lieutenant or captain that tours the unit, but in segregation, a guard usually accompanies lieutenants and captains.

Fortunately, for those seven months, I did a lot of talking with God. After being released from there, the verdict was to ship me back up north. Within a week, I was confined to my quarters again for a short span of time. Shortly thereafter, I was moved in with an elderly Indian lady, who was constantly trying to get me at odds with neighboring inmates. At the opportune time, I confronted her in front of the gang member to whom she was lying about me. She was exposed and wasn't happy about it.

A couple days later while playing the board game Scrabble, she asked to speak to me. A few of the intimates and I were playing in our cell and she hit me in the head with a lock. Surprised and taken off guard, I immediately grabbed my head with my hand and saw blood pouring from my hand, dripping onto the cement floor. Quickly, she had a mangled lip and broken nose.

To no surprise, she started banging on the door calling for the guard. Unsurprisingly, again, I was placed in solitary confinement for the remainder of my six months before my release. During confinement, I reached out and embraced the fact that God had been watching over me all of my life. I rejoiced in Him in spite of the broken places. God's grace is sufficient for your needs and your scars. For the hurting, God has intensive care. He was nurturing me through crisis situations, in solitary confinement.

There is no torment like inner torment. How can you run from yourself? If the clanging, rattling chains of old ghosts are not laid to rest, you will not have any real sense of peace and inner joy. Oftentimes, the residual effects of being abused linger for many years. Some never find deliverance because they never allow Christ to come into the dark places of their lives. Jesus has promised to set us free from every curse of the past. If you have suffered abuse, please know that He will bring you complete healing. He wants the whole person well in body, emotions, and spirit. He will deliver you from all the residue of your past. Perhaps the incident is over, but the crippling is still there. He also will deal with the crippling that's left in your life.

On July 7, 2014, I was released from prison. I headed directly to a program for parolees. After living there for a couple of months, I met my daughter's dad. This was short-lived before we got kicked out of two parole houses, due to the chaos that followed me like an invisible thread. One of the first things that a hurting person needs to do is break the habit of using other people as a narcotic to numb the dull aching of an inner void. The more you medicate the symptoms, the less chance you have of allowing God to heal you.

Once again, I was in this pandemonium cycle: moving from house to house for shelter while becoming pregnant. To make matters worse, my daughter's father was now doing crystal meth. This unhealthy relationship had twisted my judgment. Here I was, repeating a seemingly endless, chaotic cycle. Following a cesarean birth, I ended up with 22 staples, numerous stitches, and no one by my side. But, I did have this blinking, winking, squirming little slice of love, wrapped in a blanket and forever fastened to my heart. I just had a baby girl who I named Kyna.

Unfortunately, the nightmare continued. I was still on parole. Sadly, Kyna and I were homeless, and she became ill due to our living conditions. Finding ourselves again in a shelter for a six-month period was the consequence of my choices. Prior to leaving the program, they had advised me not to enter into a relationship for six months.

However, this 45-year-old gentleman and myself, 27 at the time, moved in together. Abandonment issues always brought me back to this defeated place. My boyfriend's unfaithfulness to me was exposed while I was looking through his phone. I confronted him over the issue and the retaliation exploded while in the car. Swiftly, he reached over and choked me until I saw stars. He then dragged me by both of my legs out of the car. My daughter was screaming and crying. He tried to leave, so I grabbed the keys and threw them in my yard. The neighbors observed the whole ordeal and called the police.

Both the abuser and the victim were rising into a blazing inferno. The next day, his family bailed him out and the fear gripped my heart. Fearing for my life, I went to a domestic violence shelter for 180 days.

I'm currently attending college, my daughter is adjusting, and thanks to God, we're surrounded by a strong support team. One thing that I have learned is that abuse doesn't get better if you don't do anything–it just keeps getting worse. You have to be your own friend, have compassion for yourself, forgive yourself, and know you deserve better.

Until the desire to go forward becomes greater than the memories of past pain, you will never hold the power to create again. Without a vision to go ahead, you will always live in yesterday's struggles. Today, my mom continues in and out of rehab. After giving birth to me and my sisters, Mom continued to have an additional six children, totaling 11 altogether. Sadly, all of us ended up in the foster care system, wearing scars of yesterday. My son lives with his dad, and we have frequent visits.

God wants to give each one of us the strength to overcome past pain and move forward into new life. Birthing comes through pain. Everything you bring forth comes through pain. If it didn't come through pain, it probably wasn't worth much. If you're going to bring forth a vision and purpose - you will do so with sorrow and pain. If you're going to bring forth anything in your career or marriage - it will be realized through sorrow and pain. If you're going to develop anything in your character and become a fruitful woman - it's going to come through sorrow. Some of the most productive output is produced through the things you suffer.

When you think about it, sorrow is not the object, it's simply the canal that the object comes through. Therefore, don't settle for the pain and not get the benefit. For every struggle in your life, God accomplished something in your character and in your spirit. You are holding on to the wrong thing if all you do is concentrate on past pain. I learned I had to release the pain. Pain doesn't go away on its own, it has to be released.

As we all begin to push in spite of the pain, the pain recedes into the background because we become preoccupied with the change rather than the problem. Push! You don't have time to cry. Push! You don't have time to be suicidal. Push! This is not the time to give up. Push, because God is about to birth a promise through you. Cry if you must, and groan if you have to, but keep on pushing because God has promised that if it is to come into the world, it has to pass through you.

Many attempts have come to keep us from our potential. That potential may be locked up at times because of ruined histories. God will wipe the slate clean. He will likely use others to help in the process. You have nothing to lose and everything to gain. Jesus will straighten the crooked places in your heart and make you completely whole. When you allow Him access to every area of your life, you will never be the same broken person again.

"Therefore, if anyone is in Christ, he is a new creation; the old has gone, the new has come!"
(*NIV*, 2 Cor. 5:17)

Bruised, but not broken …

Self-Reflection
Chapter 2

Circle four of the following expressions of anger you identify with the most.

Resentment	Hurt
Irritation	Disappointment
Frustration	Fury
Rage	Bugged
Agitation	Ticked-off

1. Anger is a secondary emotion. What rejection, attack, or threat might be driving your anger?

2. How has holding on to anger stunted your growth or blocked your forward movement? How has your anger affected those closest to you?

Chapter 3

WORTHY OF LOVE

While sitting in the hospital room with my mom on her deathbed, she uttered powerful words with a smile, "I love you, Amelia." Never in my life had I heard these words expressed from her mouth. What's even sadder is the fact that I never expected her to speak the word "love" directly to me.

A few days later, mom looked into my eyes without recognizing that I was her daughter and said, "Who is your mother? You are so beautiful." Once again, never had I heard Mom even compliment anyone. I wasn't sure whether to cry, laugh, or run out of the room in ultimate disillusionment. But I chose to remain at her bedside. Ultimately, looking intensely into her sunken and sickened eyes, I replied, "You are my mother." I struggled to verbalize this while allowing the emotions and adrenaline to find release through tears. Her hair was wispy, layered, and coarse. She had a small body frame, with broad shoulders, as she lay in a reclining position on the hospital bed. Her voice was faint, but her strength was coming back into her voice as she repeated, "I'm sorry, for the way I have treated you all these years." It had been 20 years since I'd seen or spoken to my mom.

Let me take you on a journey. Ralph and Johnny Ramirez were married on July 18, 1947. From their union thirteen children were born, myself being the third from the youngest. Dysfunction was our family's middle name. My parents are both now dead. Finally, I can stop denying how appallingly my brothers and, more specifically, my mother, treated me. Like the cold breeze of a grave, Mom's words seemed to cut my very soul. Throughout life, I had become her punching bag. She physically abused my body and emotionally treated me like I was made of stone. Mom rejected, ranted, and raved at me. My father was an alcoholic, therefore, he was both emotionally and physically absent during most of my childhood and teenage years. In my home, love was neither a physical nor an emotional expression you'd experience. There was no love, no attention, and no contact or bonding. For years, I was sure it was all because I was not good enough. That's what I was told.

Both of my parents had serious problems that impacted every other member of the family, so each member of the family felt compelled to adopt typical roles in order for us to survive as a whole. Mom was physically abused by Dad, and Mom's fear of not having financial provision for her children chained her to a life of continual abuse. Consequently, Mom enabled Dad to continue his unhealthy, irresponsible, and antisocial behavior. She felt powerless to do anything about it.

Growing up, I viewed dysfunction as "normal." Unfortunately, I didn't have a frame of reference for a healthy family, as we were sheltered. My family reminds me of a bunch of strings tied together tighter than what is comfortable. I'm the stray piece trying to cut loose without hands.

I was five in kindergarten when I came to the first realization that I didn't have a happy life. This is the time when a child has developed most of their motor skills; she can jump high, run, climb well, and start to do more advanced movements like ballet or gymnastics. She is comfortable with a little more independence, which means she enjoys being around family members and friends. During this time, one is able to express herself more clearly; she's able to give explanations, retell stories, and put together sentences to make herself understood.

Contrary to the positive milestones, I was a five-year-old also witnessing my dad beating my mother, and on one particular occasion, pointing a gun at her neck. In pure rage, my dad was like a wild animal with gleaming eyes, contoured face, and repeatedly blinking sweat from his eyes. Dad was cursing at Mom, yelling louder and louder. The grip he had on her, holding her to the floor, incapacitated Mom's arms, preventing her from the ability to protect herself. Wild with fear, I pulled at my dad's shirt repeatedly saying, "Please, Dad, don't hurt her!" You could see pure hate in Dad's eyes. But, he took his eyes off her for a quick moment, looked down at me, then looked back at her shouting, "If it wasn't for Amelia, you'd be a dead woman!" Mom was fearfully trembling. Stricken with silence, she ran off into the bedroom. Here I was frozen to the spot as my dad stormed out the front door.

On another occasion, one Saturday morning, Dad began his rampage of drinking. Seemingly, as each shot of liquor was drunk, his erratic behavior started to spiral downward. Everyone was acting excruciatingly kind yet feeling gray inside and out, like zombies on TV.

Once again, Dad attacked Mom, beginning with slanderous words. Quickly, it escalated to violent physical abuse. My older sister snuck into the bedroom to call the police and report the incident. By the time the police officer arrived, the commotion had eased, but broken plates and shattered glass littered the kitchen and dining areas. While trying to find a place to hide, I ended up under the dining room table. Seeing the officer's black boots from beneath the table brought comfort and fear at the same time.

Eventually, my dad left, and it would be ten years before our faces would meet again. Being extremely opinionated didn't help matters. It resulted in a slap in the face on many days. I was eight by this time with the responsibility of cleaning and washing clothes. My older siblings by this time had moved out, escaping the wrath of my mother. Throughout the years, Mom had become more bitter, drinking increasingly and looking for an excuse to take out her frustration on us kids.

To add insult to injury, my older brother and his wife had moved in with us. My dad had taught him well how to treat a wife. The vicious cycle was ever revolving. On many occasions, speaking for her defense would get me slapped or punched. On this particular occasion, it was Sunday afternoon, which was our normal movie outing time. We had plans to attend the Sunday matinee, and in the middle of their arguing, I interrupted saying, "Why are you treating her this way?" The hit to my face for responding in her defense resulted in a fierce punch to my eye, now turning black and blue. Too embarrassed to go out in public, I chose to remain home.

Shortly after they left, there was a sudden knock on the front door.

Recognizing Alex, a family friend, I opened the door. Alex walked in and saw the condition of my face and asked immediately what had happened.

"Tony hit me because I was defending his wife," I said while sobbing and trying to wipe the tears from my eyes. As tears were streaming down my face, Alex handed me a paper towel from the kitchen counter. He gripped my hand, reassuring me everything would be fine. Looking intensely at me, as if trying to read my face, Alex began to console me and offered me his apartment to relax for a few hours. At 14, I was thinking it would be a good idea and replied, "Sure, why not."

After a few hours of watching TV, I was beginning to drift in and out of sleep. Alex suggested, "It would be good if you could stay here tonight." He walked over to the refrigerator and proceeded to get some additional ice for my swollen eye. "Trust me," Alex reassured with a grim look on his face. "Please, Alex, it's time for me to go home."

Walking toward the door, Alex grabbed my arm and pushed me back onto the couch. "Hey," I hollered at the top of my voice. "What are you doing?" He forcefully responded, "You're not going anywhere." Unfortunately, Alex didn't intend to drive me home. He had other plans…

I remember very few things about the actual rape – the struggle, as well as the moment I felt too overpowered to resist any longer. In that instant, I realized there was nothing more I could do to stop what was happening. Alex was simply too strong.

When it was over, during the early morning hours, I called my mother. While hysterically crying, I said, "Mother, something bad has happened to me!" Too afraid and embarrassed to say whom I was with and what exactly occurred, the only words flooding from my mouth were, "I'm in pain."

She proceeded to call me every demoralizing name possible and insisted I don't return to her house. Mom was streaming hurtful words saying, "You got what you deserve! I curse you," she bellowed out three times. "I disown you!" I was in total shock. I remember very little about those following hours. I do recall standing in the shower with my clothes on, sobbing uncontrollably, desperately wanting the water to wash away the evening's events.

It was extremely difficult to re-adjust and cope for a period after that horrific event. The residual mental, physical, and spiritual effects of sexual assault and rape started to permeate my daily life. Effects of the sexual assault and rape came in waves.

Without anywhere to go and Alex playing manipulative mind games, I became his sex slave for the next three months. The thought of escape was futile. Whenever Alex left, he held me hostage by locking me inside the apartment. It was a complex form of trauma, breaching my physical, mental, and spiritual trust against my will. Especially being only 14 during this traumatic time, my mental stability was greatly damaged. I later found out the brain is highly adaptable during its formative years.

I built a facade around me made of sarcasm and stubbornness, where I could easily swallow my emotions.

Shortly after, I became aware I was pregnant, and the emotional roller coaster heightened. By this time, I had become numb and unresponsive as the physical abuse deepened. I remember one particular evening, sitting curled up at one end of the couch with an elbow propped on the armrest. I had red, puffy eyes and was feeling exhausted, as usual. I was also experiencing a huge headache from crying all afternoon. My stomach was in knots. It was like a nightmare. I was feeling lifeless, like there was no reprieve from the shame and humiliation hovering over me. Fortunately, nightmares come to an end, but these horrifying scenes ran like continual episodes.

Out from nowhere, Alex began saying, "You're stupid! You don't appreciate anything I've done for you!" Within seconds, I felt a strike on my head while lying huddled on my side on the couch. Wide-eyed and breathing hard, I struggled to back away when my body fell off the couch to the floor. I received hit after hit! I thought either me, my unborn child, or both of us were going to die.

"Nobody knows I'm here," I uttered softly.

"Who will rescue me?" I kept asking myself over and over again.

Kicks came one after another to my rib cage. Every jostle sent ripples of pain throughout my back. Flesh wounds from the left side of my face oozed blood, while the entire right side of my face wore a purplish-yellow smear of a bruise. Pain seared through me with intensity like a sharp-toothed creature, eating me from within. Alex jammed his knee into my side, sending shock waves of dull, nauseating pain deep into my abdomen.

Gasping for air and crying for help were useless.

Half conscious, I found myself in the back seat of the car and ended up in the emergency room parking lot.

"Get out," he screamed.

Managing to stagger through the parking lot to the hospital entrance felt like an eternity.

It was a busy Saturday night at the community hospital emergency room (ER). The crowded waiting room had a long line of people with various injuries requiring attention from the busy doctors and nurses. There was a child with a facial laceration, an older man suffering from intense lower back pain, and a young man with an apparent broken arm.

I was standing among the other patients. Intense, debilitating abdominal pain was beginning to consume my whole body. To the best of my ability, I tried to ride out the increasingly painful cramps. My stomach was bizarrely misshapen and distended. I felt shooting pains ricocheting through my body.

The waiting room patients were piled on top of one another like sardines. No one registered with an actual hospital staff member. Instead, an electronic kiosk registered waiting patients. My fellow sick patients were, in a word, depressing. I watched toothless ghosts of humans shuffle in from the street, pulling shopping carts behind them. They were standing for 10 minutes in front of a computer trying to figure out how to be helped. We sat wherever possible. The woman in the chair next to me was accompanied by her worldly possessions, all neatly folded in a laundry hamper. She was experiencing three separate schizophrenic conversations out loud with people who did not exist.

And then there was me. I waited and waited, while repeatedly being bumped for someone whose condition was more severe or for someone more obnoxious.

Consequently, agonizing, raging, and excruciating pain worsened and felt more torturous as time progressed.

Finally, my number was called, and I was escorted to a cold triage room where nurse Alice examined me. The world was spinning, and my head was pounding sharply. The physical exam consisted of gathering information and checking my body's irregularities. Nurse Alice noticed bruising on my right arm, dried-up blood around my nose, and facial scrapes.

Trembling with fear and anticipation of what was next, the streaming tears from my eyes couldn't be stopped. Simultaneously, the feeling of safety embodied my soul. I felt rescued. Bent over in pain, the humiliation and shame were apparent and couldn't be hidden from the nurse.

"If only my head would stop pounding," I thought to myself. Closing my eyes, I wondered, "How could I have arrived at this strange, dark place, where nothing seemed familiar?"

Nurse Alice asked me a series of questions. However, I didn't know how to answer, as I looked down in utter disbelief. I could feel Nurse Alice's eyes glued to my lips, waiting for an answer. My heart was pounding like a jackhammer against my chest.

"Being silent was my only protection," I thought to myself.

My fingers clutching to the sheets surrounding my body felt like the hands of my angel. Certainly… at least for a few more moments.

Abruptly, there was a knock on the ER door, and the nurse invited them in the room. The lab technician had come to draw blood for various tests. By this time, hemorrhaging had sufficiently increased and it was suspected I had suffered a miscarriage.

The doctor later told me, "I'm surprised you survived the beating."

After a series of examinations, blood results, and an ultrasound, the prognosis was indeed accurate regarding the miscarriage.

By this time, a detective arrived to conduct a formal investigation. She introduced herself as Detective Edwards. We exchanged smiles and a gentle handshake. The briefest shake of my head led to tears streaming from my cheeks onto the blue-and-white top of the hospital gown. Detective Edwards was intentional in every word that she spoke. Her posture was strong, and her dark, piercing eyes stared me right in the face.

For the first time in my life, I was confronted with a strong, confident woman.

During elementary school, I thought possessing strength meant being picked first for the kickball team, even though I kicked like a girl. I believed strength meant scrunching my nose and curling my lips when a boy wanted to kiss. I also thought to be strong meant getting as dirty and hurt as the guys I played with during recess.

When I was in middle school, my perception of strength meant playing basketball, volleyball, softball, and running track. I thought demonstrating strength meant enjoying video games, heavy metal, and acting more masculine than feminine.

When I was in high school, I thought to be a strong woman meant knowing exactly what I wanted to do once I received my diploma, and not allowing a boyfriend to influence my future plans.

But what I learned from Detective Edwards on that fateful day, while sitting in a cold, emergency room, feeling ashamed and broken, put me on a search for inner strength. The lesson I learned years later is that being a strong woman means being unapologetically, fiercely, and wholeheartedly you.

I had a long way to go.

As Detective Edwards asked, "Can you tell me where you've been? Who did this to you, Amelia?" It was as if my mouth was tied shut. I had lost my power to speak up for myself. My upset came not only from my outside reality but from my inner conditioning. Remove the conditioning and the upset disappears. My way of thinking, perception, principles, and judgment were a result of the long conditioning, whereby I had adapted to and created this mental, family, and societal framework. That framework has shaped my mind, further determining how I must react to facts and situations.

Not knowing at 14 my true feelings, maturity has defined it as defeated, defective, deserted, and deprived.

Detective Edwards' curiosity and instinct were evident in her questioning. She wasn't going to leave any stone unturned in trying to get to the bottom of this case. My answers were only, "Yes," and "No," or a shrug of the shoulder. Consequently, after two hours of her not getting concrete answers, she said, "We'll have to call your family to pick you up. Because you are under age, we aren't legally able to release you on your own." It was a no-brainer, the only person I felt safe to pick me up was my older sister.

Monica had become like a mom to me, even though she moved out the house, and was living with her family. While sitting in the hospital room, Detective Edwards excused herself to call Monica. As I was looking up at the ceiling and the four surrounding walls of that orderly room, I suddenly felt like the walls were caving in on me. I was extremely shaky, desperate, and hopeless. I believed that, despite anything I did, life would never get better. There wasn't anywhere to pace around the room or distract me from suffocating in my own sorrow. Therefore, I sat absolutely still and glued to the chair.

Within minutes, Detective Edwards returned to the room with a slight smile on her face. "Your sister Monica will be picking you up shortly." Immediately, I started to gather my thoughts and plan my answers. Obviously, the first question would be, "Where have you been?" The mere thought of the last three months of my life was gut-wrenching.

"Would she believe me?" I pondered over and over, waiting for an answer that was inconceivable.

Suddenly, Monica walked in the room. She grabbed me tight and started sobbing furiously. Monica has always been my angel on earth. I love my sister because she has been everything to me that my mom lacked. We bonded over games, late night movies, pillow fighting, and making fun of Mom and Dad. Monica was like a magical mirror, exposing our true inner beings.

"Let's go," she said. Never in a million years, would I have imagined that statement as the first thing out of Monica's mouth. She had signed the discharge papers prior to entering the room, and we quickly left the emergency room.

"You are kind of quiet," Monica mentioned as we settled into the car.

Monica turned the key and backed out the parking stall. I fastened my seat belt.

By this time, Monica pulled into traffic. "Okay, so do you want to talk?" Uncertain of where to begin, I nodded with an obvious, "Yes." Monica turned to look at me. "We've been looking for you. As a matter of fact, Mom filled out a missing person's report on you a few days after you were gone."

Christmas shoppers were out in full force, and traffic was at a standstill. We weren't moving more than a car length or two with each signal change. Monica felt her frustration growing, impatient with the world, and forced herself to take a couple of deep breaths.

She rested her head back, wondering when traffic was going to move again while still waiting on my answer. Monica offered a grim smile. "We've got to talk." I felt Monica's hand cover mine, and I silently accepted the comfort.

By the time we arrived at her house, we were sobbing tears of relief. I immediately went to bed after Monica informed me she would contact Mom in the morning and let her know that I was at her house and recuperating. The doctor had ordered bed rest for a couple of days and a follow-up appointment was scheduled in seven days. Afterward, I would be released to return to school.

The following years were like attempting to chase a life I had lost. It was similar to trying to find a needle in a haystack.

Consequently, after being disowned by my mother, I began abusing drugs when I was 14. It first started with marijuana and later evolved to crystal meth.

For months afterward, when I opened my eyes in the morning, it was still dark. Half-asleep, I would get out of bed and enter the bathroom. As I emptied my bladder, I checked my face in the mirror. For an instant, I couldn't recognize my own reflection. However, I realized it was my reflection after seeing the person wave back whenever I waved my hand. My life had been altered into broken pieces. Sometimes, it can seem impossible to repair the broken pieces.

During the summer, families would occasionally gather for Saturday afternoon barbeques. By this time, I was 15 and hadn't seen my father in seven years.

Unfortunately, I'm part of that statistic of fatherless girls. All my siblings were eager to see Dad, as he was invited to one of our family gatherings. As I have gotten older and more comfortable in my own skin, I have recognized my need to heal from certain issues in order to move forward. Getting over daddy issues definitely requires healing. But let me ask you: Do you ever really get over your daddy issues?

There is no stage in life where you can "get over" not having a father.

I'm reminded of it when I look back on my past friendships and recall seeing my best friend have date nights with her father. It's a constant pain that faintly throbs and then spikes when various situations arise. If I could take a painkiller, I would, but nothing changes the heartache of a fatherless girl.

The "reunion day" arrived. My reaction was nothing I had contemplated. For days I had dreamed of an awesome, liberating reunion. But on the contrary, it was the complete opposite. The moment I set eyes on my dad, feelings of anger and hostility overtook me. With detest in my eyes, rage began deepening. I started pounding on his chest, asking, "Why did you leave me?" All I could envision were images of pain, lonely nights, and years of questioning why I wasn't enough.

While I was working to forgive him and my mother for being human, the question remains: How on earth could he abandon me?

Besides, I needed him and he didn't care. How does one sleep at night not knowing if his own flesh-and-blood was breathing, eating, safe, and secure? My pain runs deep, just like it did for my other brothers and sisters. Dad brought dysfunction into my life. He was the first man to break my heart, and I struggled not to hate him.

The words that flowed out of his mouth were, "I'm sorry." But they were void of truth and felt empty. They were words with no substance.

The anticipation of a grand reunion was short-lived. Once again, disappointment set in. Unfortunately, things weren't going well at my sister's house. My family members, especially those in close proximity, had constant access to my life.

The mentality that influences one's approach to situations, circumstances, and challenges has a way of bleeding into your subconscious. Consequently, the outlook was negative. Therefore, the house was full of chaos, and I was forced to move out.

I found myself living on the streets wherever I could find shelter. At 15, with no further education, I needed a job to provide for myself. Monica assisted me in getting a job at an abortion clinic as a receptionist. The owner of the clinic thought I was 18 and allowed me to work full-time. She rented me an apartment she owned, and I was finally off the streets. It took weeks before I actually realized this was an abortion clinic. While working one particular day, I noticed a clear specimen jar on a shelf. It contained tiny fingers inside. Lashing out in ultimate disbelief, I burst into the owner's office shouting, "How could you be killing these babies?"

Storming out of the office with no place to work, I found myself at Carl's Jr. completing a job application. My consistent work ethic afforded me the opportunity to move up the ranks and eventually become a supervisor by the time I was 17.

It was here that I thought I had met the man of my dreams. "Ricky" walked into the restaurant with a loose black T-shirt and blue jeans. However, Ricky looked more handsome the longer I stared. His rich, chocolate hair had tousled griminess that promised finesse. Ricky had strong, arched brows and eyelashes so thick it could be illegal. And then, his vivid, light brown eyes – were beautiful and captivating. Ricky had distinct cheekbones and an angular jaw. His pale skin made him look devilishly handsome. Surely, he was "the one."

We dated for a short period of time before we married. Within three months of our marriage, the physical abuse commenced, and within six months, I was pregnant. Ricky started doing drugs, and his total behavior changed. His relentless accusations, callous and absurd, would lead to violent arguments. Many days, my eyes would be puffy, swollen, and have mascara smudges from tears. Almost daily, my once rosy cheeks now appeared flushed, seemingly worn down and tired.

Ricky came home one evening overly intoxicated. It was as if he was on a mission to destroy my life. His eyelids were swollen nearly shut, and his hair was falling from the front of his forehead in thin clusters. Ricky tried to say something, but it came out as nothing but a guttural bark. His face was emotionless as he circled around me like predators hunting down prey. I looked at him, begging and pleading. I couldn't handle it anymore. "Shut up! Just shut up!" he cursed and looked at me with rage. "Look what you made me do!"

My husband used his malicious authority to kick me out the house that evening. On yet another occasion, I was stranded with no car. I didn't know how to function in a world without chaos and violence.

After packing a small suitcase for my small son, I went to my mom's house to escape from danger, or so I thought.

I looked raggedy arriving at my mom's house in desperation. My hair was windblown due to the high winds, and my voice was croaky. As Mom opened the door, she looked somewhat surprised to see me and the baby. Reluctantly, she invited us in, and I flopped onto the couch. I asked, "Mom, is it okay if we stay here for a little while? We have nowhere else to go." With a nod of her head she replied, "Sure, but you'll have to find a place on the floor to sleep."

Not asking any questions, she looked back at the baby as she walked off to her bedroom.

I had subjected my life to five years of abuse. Ricky's harassment continued by calling me with threats if I didn't allow him to see his son. Three days later, Ricky appeared at my mother's house. "Why are you hiding my son from me?" The argument escalated. My brother came to Ricky's defense saying, "Don't let her talk to you like that!" Before I knew it, my brother slapped me to the ground and kicked me like I was a soccer ball. Mom was laughing while looking down at me, getting joy and satisfaction from seeing her daughter being abused.

As I took deep breaths, it hurt my ribcage. I exhaled, inhaled and struggled to push myself onto my hands and knees. My head swirled in pain. I felt my stomach tighten and I threw up, which increased the pain in my ribs. I remained in this position for a bit: on my hands and knees with my head hanging, like a winded horse.

It would be 20 years before I would see my mom ever again – until she was lying in the hospital bed.

Never did I experience a warm, loving family. But, hurting people can only love you on their terms. Because of the trauma I experienced,

I grew up missing the important parts of necessary parenting that prepared me for adulthood.

Shortly following those defeating days, I could be conquered by the smallest obstacle: a hard-to-open jar, bad news, or a dead battery in my car. I couldn't get out of bed, sleeping ten, eleven, or twelve hours at a time. Or, I had insomnia and couldn't sleep at all, spending my nights flipping the TV channel from infomercials to televangelists to seedy cop dramas.

Later, I understood that as an adult, you carry the memories of your past. My experience has shaped and molded me in countless ways that remain deeply buried in my subconscious. The past left its scars, painful wounds, emotional pain, and confusion. Life statements replay like endless mental recordings in my mind.

These statements say, "You're not good enough! It's impossible to succeed!"

I eventually divorced Ricky and made peace with my parents and family members. The hole in my heart must be replaced and filled with new experiences. Are you filling the void with other things instead of breaking free from what has been chasing you all these years?

When you are empty, you try to fill the void with things: money, relationships, work, or whatever gives you a sense of satisfaction.

Growing up with abuse of every kind and being rejected and discarded by my family crushed my spirit at a very early age. Sadness and despair evolved into anger and rage. I became self-destructive, turning to drugs after experiencing sexual abuse. Drugs severely aggravated my frail state of mind to the point of suicidal thoughts. The roller coaster ride of doing drugs from 14 to 21, and then again from 25 to 38 took its toll on my life. After finally hitting rock bottom, I called out from the depths of my soul to a God I didn't know personally but had heard about. Our God in His great mercy heard my cry. I had an encounter with the King of Kings and Lord of Lords. After I started meditating on His Word, chains began to break and scars began to heal.

God filled my heart with love and forgiveness and taught me that I am who He says I am and that I can do what He says I can do! This truth set me free from bondage, and in His faithfulness, He lifted me out of the gutter and gave me a new identity. No longer was I an orphan, for I had become adopted by the Blood of Jesus. The scripture says, "When your mother and father forsake you, then the Lord will take you up." That scripture had become a reality for me.

I now understand why the attacks on my soul were so strong. God has a tremendous calling on my life. The enemy is under my feet and has no power over me, because greater is my Lord that is inside of me. I've been sober for 11 years and intend to remain this way for the rest of my life.

Furthermore, because the Lord has equipped and entrusted me with spiritual gifts, I will be able to empower those who are lost, hurt, and desolated, reassuring them that if God did it for me, He will surely do it for them!

Coming to know Jesus has made it all worthwhile. As I stand on the promise that, "My latter days will be better than my former years," saith the Lord.

Each of our stories show up in our relationships. And we wonder, "How did I get to this place again: satisfying others, more than self, and what is the circle of my chaos?"

However, each one of us must also realize that when we make a choice to stay in our story, we create a glass ceiling over our head. The construction worker *you* called placed this blockage there.

Freedom starts from the point of us being able to talk about our past. The story behind the incident sometimes has a way of causing you to repeat old habits, and old habits stand in the way, oftentimes stopping you from achieving your goals. People are afraid to give up their story, believing they are giving away power. In actuality, they are empowering themselves.

Now, I can stand back as though observing myself and say, "My belief in God hasn't changed. My expectation that God would help hasn't wavered." I was simply standing in a storm so ferocious I couldn't find words to form a prayer. I could only look up saying, "Oh, God, my God!"

"Though I walk through the valley of the shadow of death, I will fear no evil. Thy rod and thy staff comfort me..." The words shimmered like a faint melody, unsought, just there.

Life experiences and stories shape who you are. Sometimes, they make you feel as though you're not good enough. Your stories are a mixture of thoughts and emotions that affect you.

There is a champion in you fighting to emerge. Let her out! Release her from the nest, and allow her to develop her own wings. Let her be her unapologetically authentic self.

Sometimes, you will have to fight yourself for your life! You are your own hero!

Bruised, but not broken ...

Self-Reflection
Chapter 3

1. How have your wounds influenced your emotional and spiritual growth?

2. How has your hurt made you more compassionate and sensitive? What types of people in pain do you find yourself particularly drawn to?

3. Identify something positive about your life. Celebrate! Remind yourself that good things are still happening.

Chapter 4

STOLEN INNOCENCE

B orn with fluid on my brain in 1954, it was not the most advantageous of circumstances – to say the least. Back then, doctors were puzzled and diagnosed my condition as hydrocephalus. It is a brain condition that occurs when cerebrospinal fluid (CSF) cannot drain from the brain. CSF is the clear, watery fluid that surrounds and cushions the brain and spinal cord. At the time, my parents were told if CSF wasn't treated, it could lead to brain damage, a loss of mental and physical abilities, and even death. Thankfully, the doctors successfully treated the condition. The minimally-invasive approach involved placing a small, lighted camera inside my brain so surgeons could view the surgical site on a computer monitor. Then, while using very small instruments, surgeons made a tiny hole in the bottom of my brain. This hole created an "evacuation route," which released the fluid from my brain.

What a grand way to begin life!

I recall growing up in Los Angeles, South Central to be exact. Tough, rough, and violent would be the description of my neighborhood. It consisted of poor, lower-class, working people, just trying to make a living on a nominal income. With Mom holding down two jobs and Dad working a full-time job, there wasn't anyone left at home to fill in the gap for me and my nine siblings. As the second oldest, I was responsible for my younger siblings. Somehow, I also inherited the "Mom #2" position in the house. I didn't ask or volunteer for this job. Nevertheless, the duty was dropped in my lap.

My father was an alcoholic. Walking into a room where Dad was passed out on the couch with the TV playing was a routine occurrence. You simply ignored Dad, turned off the TV, and went to bed. Gradually, I came to terms with the fact that it was my responsibility to tuck him in at night and not the other way around. As a child, situations like this happened so frequently that I no longer flinched at the sight of empty beer bottles scattered around the living room. But, I didn't dare have friends visit. As much as I had a good time playing with dolls and having tea parties with the neighborhood girls, my house was off-bounds. It was much easier to visit another friend's house as opposed to mine. Whenever friends did visit, the day would usually end awfully. Dad would inevitably stumble around and crack inappropriate jokes. Although you couldn't quite understand Dad's humor, it always left a nasty feeling in the pit of one's belly.

Shortly after I turned 10, things progressively worsened. Consequently, not only was I "Mom #2" to my younger siblings, but I also became "Wife #2" to my dad. Yes, you heard it right. Dad started conducting inappropriate behavior with me. I was scared to tell anyone; I thought it was my fault because I didn't stop him. But, he threatened me. I felt like I couldn't tell anyone. I didn't know what to do. I didn't want anyone at school finding out because I thought they'd all look down on me.

More and more, the level of sexual acts intensified ferociously. Unfortunately, fondling escalated to sexual penetration. At 10 years old, I lost my virginity—to my father. While lying on a sheet of blood-patched spots, the uncertainty of what took place surrounded my mind. My ears were ringing. All I could hear was Dad's strong, authoritative voice. He was commanding, "Get up! Clean yourself up. You're going to be alright." Although feeling groggy and numb, I attempted to clean every bodily substance that was left behind. I found myself running into the bathroom and hopping into the tub. Looking down at the bloody water, I wondered if it would ever disappear. I had no clue as to what was happening to my body. As a child, this kind of physical and emotional pain became overwhelming.

At this moment, I was confronted with a sense of angst, alienation, and despair, moving from mild to severe. Every part of my body tensed up while stepping out of the tub, one-foot-at-a-time, onto the old, stained floor. Drying the remaining water off my immature, fragile, lifeless body seemed to take a lifetime. Despite my bathing efforts, it felt like an invisible stain covered my skin. This invisible mark would forever haunt me.

My dad's imagination grew increasingly corrupted. He was no longer satisfied with just one daughter fulfilling his devilish sexual cravings. Instead, he now insisted that my older half-sister was added to the demoralizing acts. One-by-one, he would signal us to go into the bathroom while he sat on the covered toilet seat and we sat on the floor. Dad instructed us to perform every possible unimaginable sexual act. From age 10 to 12, my dad tortured me with horrendous behavior.

During this time, Dad established a maddening ability to pretend nothing happened afterward. Of course, we never whispered a word to anyone. This secret was something my half-sister and I thought we'd never tell anyone else nor discuss with each other. Besides, who would believe two little adolescents from South Central L.A.? However, as my sister and I looked into each other's eyes, we saw the pain, hurt, and embarrassment we thought we'd hidden. Buried beneath neat ponytails, fancy hair ribbons, and pretty dresses, two souls had been severely damaged by unspeakable trauma. For some unforeseen reason, my half-sister was sent away to stay with relatives. Now, I was left alone to endure two years of incest from my natural father.

I resented my mother – the woman who had birthed me into the world. I felt like she was emotionally deserting me and leaving me in the destructive hands of her husband. She wanted to leave him and move away. Mom was willing to go anywhere, but she couldn't. Mom appeared trapped. Before leaving for work, I could sense desperation in her eyes. Whenever I looked at her sitting by the door in her dated red coat, her eyes welled up with tears. Many times, she'd clasp my hands into hers and bow her head. If I could have read her thoughts, I'm sure she was saying, "Sorry, Momma has to go to work." After hastily picking up her purse, she'd rush out the door.

Clearly, I was feeling victimized by my relationship with both parents. It often felt like I was nothing more than a helpless child.

The beatings that Mom experienced from Dad caused her to make a pivotal change in our living conditions. Finally, my mother decided, "Enough is enough." On a Monday morning, while Dad was at work, Mom surreptitiously filled a suitcase with her clothes, shoes, and toiletries. She gathered as many of our belongings as she could place in a few garbage bags. As we hurried to the train station, we exclaimed, "Mom, we don't have all our stuff." Mom's intense facial expressions spoke volumes. She replied, "Some things just aren't important." Although not fully comprehending her response, we hunched our shoulders and replied, "OK, Momma." Quickly, we stepped onto the train, making sure everyone was present.

Traveling to North Carolina was adventurous. MaDear, my grandmother, would be waiting for us after the exciting but tiring twelve-hour ride. For me, the very sight of MaDear brought a sigh of relief. Her slender physique with broad shoulders and piercing, dark-brown eyes portrayed strength and beauty simultaneously. Her voice sounded gentle and courageous within the same breath.

All of us crowded in a small three-bedroom house with MaDear. At times, sharing one bathroom with seven siblings was quite unbearable. We ate in shifts, so we could take turns sitting at the kitchen table. Hoping and praying enough food was left when it came to my turn was a normal occurrence. Boy, do I remember Saturday mornings and the delicious smell of crispy, Southern fried chicken, fluffy homemade buttermilk biscuits, and dark country gravy. To top it off, MaDear would make a mouth-watering homemade pound cake! You see, MaDear was what you call "old school," she wasn't one for using a bunch of mushy words. For me, cooking was one of her many ways of demonstrating love.

During this time, my "prayer muscles" also developed. Producing a consciousness of God began at MaDear's house. Every morning and evening, MaDear would gather us to recite the Lord's Prayer. Within a few months, we no longer needed MaDear's help with recitation. The prayer easily flowed from our lips like harmonious melodies of music.

For the first time in my life, I experienced a sense of normalcy. It was a relief not waking in the middle of the night by slamming doors, Dad's footsteps roaming throughout the house, and Mom crying (sometimes screaming) or gasping for dear life. I was no longer feeling worthless or like an insignificant human due to sexual torment. No longer was I being hunted by my father like a piece of meat in the forest.

Yes, life was feeling good until the age of eighteen. Consequently, you can't escape the scars of the past. Some scars have a way of lingering despite healing. Sadly, the aftermath of being a fatherless girl was beginning to emerge from a space in my heart I assumed had been sealed off from all humanity. I was a fatherless girl. And it's supposed to be the responsibility of a father to teach his daughter how to behave in a nonsexual, intimate relationship with a man prior to marriage. But, when I was 10, my father taught me it's acceptable to be violated under the guise of a father's love. Fathers are a mirror to their daughter, reflecting positive self-esteem for a girl to embrace. Girls nurtured and loved by their fathers know their worth comes from what's between their ears and not what's between their legs. Unfortunately, in my house, it was the very opposite.

Therefore, never receiving affirmation from my father left me the prey of an older man. He was 12 years my senior. Subsequently, as a fatherless young lady, I started a relationship that would forever alter my life. Drugs, alcohol, and prostitution placed debilitating crutches on me. And from the age of 18 to 30, I became a slave to self-destructive behavior. Chasing cocaine highs, selling it, and prostituting my body was a "normal" way of life. I would often ask myself, "How can I be so naive?" But, my cries seemed to be ricocheting off the walls.

On frequent flights from California to Salt Lake City, Utah, my prayer muscles were exercised. Going through the airport terminal checkpoints with bags of cocaine tucked away on my body was the scariest part of the trip. It was unnerving not knowing if the cocaine had been detected or if armed detectives were waiting for me. As the "delivery girl," I was paid royally. Someway, MaDear's prayers covered me. Besides, prior to every trip, MaDear would pray, "Lord, Jesus, protect my granddaughter, and bring her back safely." You see, I didn't keep any secrets from her. She was my only true confidant – my earthly angel. Plus, she was fully aware of my one-night stands, as well as my drug and alcohol abuse and obviously neurotic behavior. MaDear was truly the only safe person in the world I could trust.

While sitting on the couch one evening snorting cocaine, I experienced a sudden flashback. In the flashback, I re-experienced the original abuse. I remembered emotions I felt at the time Dad was fondling me. Remembering him reaching up my skirt was like watching a movie about someone else's life. Vividly, I saw his "private parts" coming toward me and the big black belt he always wore.

One night, a few years prior, this was the same experience that I faced with a "john." It was like viewing slides in a presentation when the slides appear extremely fast but slow enough to provide a glimpse of the image. That horrendous flashback was very vivid; enough of the feelings were sneaking in that I knew it wasn't a dream.

To add insult to my already crazy life, my boyfriend constantly badgered me about not really needing me in his life. His demeaning words cut like a knife, piercing my already bruised heart. Besides, I was only 18 and he was 30 years old. His continual manipulation and mind games were taking a toll on me, not to mention the continual physical abuse, now occurring regularly. The pattern of abuse became predictable. I would be slapped, snatched up, or thrown across the room once he had indulged in some Jim Beam Bourbon Whiskey and Valium.

During this time, my boyfriend was making quite a bit of money dealing drugs. He looked for reasons to emotionally abuse me. I was often ridiculed for not being able to read. Let's face it. While helping raise my seven siblings, education was not at the top of my daily list of chores.

I clearly remember one particular evening when my boyfriend was experiencing one of his tantrums. The apartment door swung open, and he entered the house like a wild, untamed animal, ready to attack his prey. While he was looking for an excuse to attack me once again, I sat quietly determined to not say a word. However, beneath my breath, I whispered, "Lord, help me." Before I knew it, he quickly reached the kitchen entrance, where I was sitting. That day, not only did I stand up from that chair, but my spirit roared like a lion! For the very first time, I experienced an inner strength I never knew existed. Surprisingly, to my own hearing, powerful words flowed from my mouth. I challenged him, "What could you ever do to me that will measure up to the pain I've already experienced?"

Not quite sure where the strength came from, I heard myself saying, "Not today! Not anymore." While making my way to the knives on the counter, I knew today was the day I'd either walk into the jailhouse or out of his nasty old house. The choice was his, and I was definitely up for the challenge. Obviously, God was at work. Slowly, I emerged from the ashes of despair. That was the last day he ever lifted a hand at me! It was also the first day I opened the door of my caged soul. I freed myself.

By this time, MaDear was growing older, and her fragile body was increasingly deteriorating. She could no longer sit on the front porch of her house talking and watching neighbors enter and exit their homes. Nor could she enjoy hours of conversation sparked from spontaneous discussions with walkers who passed her porch. Gradually, it was becoming more difficult for MaDear to catch up on all the neighborhood gossip and get life updates on family members, friends, and a few enemies.

In 1982, MaDear died of a massive heart attack. The matriarch of our family, MaDear, lived life standing tall in the face of adversity. She was an admirable woman who died with great dignity. Never whimpering the slightest or uttering a word of complaint about her challenges, MaDear chose to make the best out of her life. If she ever had any regrets, they were never expressed. She often called me "baby girl," and whispered gems of wisdom like, "Elegance is an inside job: the outside stuff is how you celebrate your elegance." I'd nod a silent understanding. MaDear's precious prayers had brought me this far, but my prayers would lead me further.

During this time in my life, I was ready to confront Mother about our bruised past. Before I told her about the incest, I believed she would provide unconditional love and nurturing. Afterward, I had to tear down those false assumptions and replace them with a harsh reality check.

I needed to put on my "big girl panties" and deal with her. Mom came up with every possible excuse as to why she didn't have a clue what had happened to me. My narcissistic mother constantly diverted the discussion back to her. There was no trace of empathy for my feelings. Mom would usually respond saying, "What do you want me to do? Your dad is dead now!" That statement alone brought up more unimaginable feelings. Not being able to confront him was another unmet need. Repeatedly, I was robbed of voicing my emotions. Experiencing the memory feeling detached, helpless, terrified, and in physical pain can be as real as any actual experience. It was time to get off the "repeat cycle" of feeling crushed, ripped-open, and suffocated.

Finally, I resolved that Mom didn't have the capacity to confront this painful past. Nor, for once in her life, did she acknowledge the need to rescue her child. Therefore, I was left to work through resentments toward my parents and the hatred against my father. I wanted to kill him, but he was already dead. I always thought of myself as this "nice girl." However, deep inside my core, an ax-murderer existed – someone I tried for years to ignore. Now, it's time to deal with this angry personality.

Giving up a little girl's longing for security and protection was excruciating. Stepping outside of the shared beliefs of my family system and insisting on truth was frightening. I felt like a lonely speck of dust floating in a big, empty world. I was constantly on the roller coaster of life. Its variations of turns, spins, highs, and lows were all

I could imagine, and I needed hope for my life. Life hadn't been fair to me.

I thought, "Why was I dealt such a bad deck of cards? Why had I become the punching bag for men to vent their frustration? What invisible sign hung on my head that invited these predators to identify me as their next bait?" These questions rolled from my lips, but still, no answer could be heard. I searched the mirror attempting to find any answer, but the mirror never replied. Still, no answer could be heard.

In September 2011, while again feeling unloved and undesired, another man walked out of my life. Looking at me in a detestable manner, he blurted out, "I'm gonna leave you the way I found you!" Here I was again in a seemingly familiar situation. It was like a broken record on a stereo, constantly repeating the words and the music. How could I survive? The mere thought of death looked inviting. We were once engaged when a pebble of hope had emerged. Now, countless thoughts filled my mind. How would I explain our breakup to a handful of friends? What would they think of me?

Living with no food or job, desperation became my best friend. Despair causes you to search for the Greater One. My head was swimming and my heart was sinking. I started praying and screaming out to God. While lying flat on my apartment floor, I cried out to God, "Why me? I'm a good person!"

Sobbing uncontrollably, I made God a promise: I would live for Him. Immediately, on the wall in my bedroom, Jesus appeared with blood flowing from his body. The disciples were at His feet.

I stilled myself to hear God and the answer bearing down on me like boulders in an avalanche.

In this stillness, something amazing occurred. A great voice consumed my thoughts saying, "It's time for you not to exist, but live in me!" I was now feeling a mixture of thankfulness, conviction, surrender and yet, a certain amount of fear.

Thankfully, I pondered on my new circumstance. I would no longer be a victim of my past. Although we often fail to recognize it as such, this is an essential part of the gospel. Seeing Christ's work of salvation is greater than we realize. Christ came to heal us of our wounds and set us free from all binding shackles.

There is no question we are influenced by our life experiences, and these experiences inevitably involve physical pain and emotional injury, but that is not the final word on the matter. Just because you've been unfairly treated doesn't mean you'll be doomed to a lifetime of struggle or that you'll become emotionally crippled. Just because you've been hurt by others doesn't mean you must dwell in bondage, embracing the pain and anger associated with those sufferings.

The tragedy is that numerous people refuse to believe freedom is possible! So, they continue living in bondage tied to their damaged past. Many who've experienced horrific pasts don't believe they can be set free from the tyrannizing effects of past hurts. Oftentimes, they're not ready to forgive those who've hurt them. Consequently, those hurting cling to anger and continue to embrace pain.

Nothing has the capacity to destroy us from within in quite the way hate manifests. Withholding forgiveness is embracing hatred, therefore, it is accepting our own destruction. Unfortunately, this is what I had done for years. If I continued to wait for the circumstances to be just right, I would have never forgiven my father. Or, if I would've waited until I received all the answers to my countless questions about intensely hurting, I would've never forgiven Dad. Besides, forgiveness is always offered in the midst of confusion and ambivalence.

When searching my heart for forgiveness, I decided to write down exactly what I needed to forgive. The focus of my forgiveness centered on what my father did to me and not his position in my life. We should not try to forgive someone for being obnoxious, selfish, or evil. Personality does not require forgiveness. Instead, the challenge is in forgiving one's behavior. What I determined to do was forgive my father for the specific things he did to hurt me. One-by-one, I wrote down those hurtful acts.

Many times, forgiving someone is the hardest thing a human can ever be asked to do.

Nevertheless, complete and perfect forgiveness is available to all of us through God. My own offerings of forgiveness need not be limited by past experiences. God's forgiveness of me can serve as both a model and as a resource for my own forgiveness of others.

A perfect, Heavenly Father stands ready and willing to forgive me each and every time I come to Him requesting such forgiveness. Having freely received it, I can more freely give.

Thankfully, finally, I had come to a place of reliance on God. A basic shift in my personal growth started to emerge after forgiving my parents, especially my father, and releasing the resentment. As I was lying on the floor directly after a women's group at my church, the healing started to flow. I was surrounded by praying women, who were earthly angels God assigned on my behalf. This led me out of the locked prison doors I had erected in my soul. Instantly, a flashback of Jesus on the cross and His spilled blood gave me the assurance He had done it all for me.

Week by week, I built my spiritual muscles. Participating in praise and worship, reading my Bible, and becoming a student of the Word shifted my life. My dependency on God had taken centerstage. Finally, the seeds of unforgiveness and betrayal started to empty from an invisible bag that had been tucked away in the deep crevices of my soul. Today, they are still leaking out, little-by-little. The picture of who I really am in God is becoming clearer and clearer each day. My life looks nothing like my past. Next year, my life will look nothing like it appears now.

Bruised, but not broken…

Self-Reflection

Chapter 4

God's mercies are new every morning. What challenges are you facing today in which you need God's mercy? Talk openly with Him about these concerns and invite Him to meet your specific needs.

1. As you look back over your life, when have you experienced new beginnings and evidence of God's restoration?

2. God often uses our wounds as a springboard for helping others. Write a letter to someone in pain telling them how God has transformed you through your darkest times in life.

Chapter 5

A STORMY SEASON

Have you ever experienced a life-changing moment that left you breathless? Were you rocked to your core? I've heard everybody will experience at least one tragic circumstance that questions his or her faith. Unfortunately, there's another group that endures hurricane seasons, wandering from one "bad situation" to the next. Sadly, I'm a member of the second group. I've experienced a few too many storms that have challenged my faith. Here's my story.

I received a call from my mom that shook the very foundation of my being. "Brae," my mom said frantically, "I just found Ebony hanging from the bathroom shower!" My heart dropped to the pit of my gut. I felt like I'd just been pummeled by a diesel truck. My head started ringing. I didn't know if I should believe what I was hearing, throw the phone down, or run out of the house screaming. With tears streaming down, a lump filled the bottom of my throat. All sorts of thoughts had my mind spinning. But, my mom hung up before I could ask any questions. Looking around disoriented, I struggled to gather my thoughts. I couldn't breathe. My heart was panting, racing like a thousand beats per minute. I collapsed on my living room floor, crying uncontrollably. "Is this true?" I asked myself between deep sobs.

I had raised Ebony, my little sister, as my own child. She was only fifteen years old. I was an expectant mom, all the bit of eight months pregnant with my son. Surely, I was in no condition to mentally, emotionally, or physically comprehend this horrific news. Yet, I found myself wildly running throughout the house – from room-to-room, trying to locate my husband. I couldn't find him quickly enough to tell him this devastating news.

After locating him outside, I could barely utter the words, "Ebony hung herself." Willie, my husband, was astonished. He was quiet for a moment before tearfully asking, "What are you talking about?" I proceeded to tell him about the call I just received from my mom. We immediately started gathering car keys, my purse, and other incidentals before deciding to head toward my mom's house. Prior to reaching the door, the phone rang again. Although the call was from my mom's number, an unrecognizable voice started speaking. "This is Val, your mom's downstairs neighbor. She asked me to let you know the paramedics have arrived. They're minutes away from putting Ebony in the ambulance. They're on the way to Memorial Hospital. So, get there as soon as you can!" I still couldn't believe what just happened. Time was ticking.

Finally collecting my purse and car keys, we dashed out of the kitchen door, which led to the garage. Quickly zooming backward without considering nearby cars, we backed out of the driveway and dashed down the street. After glancing at the nearby corner, we drove going north on the freeway. This was the longest twenty-minute drive you could ever imagine. Fortunately, I assumed Ebony was still alive since they were on their way to the hospital. Looking at my phone, expecting it to ring at any moment while contemplating whether or not to call my mom, and holding my stomach as a way of comforting my unborn son, I was a wreck. While praying all the way to the hospital, my stomach twisted in knots. Sweating considerably, my hands were trembling, and my head was throbbing.

Upon entering the hospital emergency doors, my stomach painfully tightened. Fear of the unknown was grasping every emotion. With medical equipment beeping and instructions hurled between doctors and nurses, I heard the close border between life and death. I saw stifled tears during serious family conversations. Groans and whispers about patients echoed the lobby.

"How is she?" I asked my mom after spotting her leaning against a wall, which was supporting her seemingly exhausted body. My frail-looking mom slightly turned her head answering, "The doctor is with her." My adrenaline was rising with the fear of possibly never seeing my sister alive again.

The doctor stepped out from behind the curtain where Ebony's body lay comatose. Although unresponsive, Ebony was alive due to the massive amount of machines maintaining her breathing. Dr. Graham desired to update us, asking if we could go somewhere private to talk. It felt like I was walking a marathon, heading toward the waiting room. It seemed an eternity. Dr. Graham led the way. My mom followed a few steps behind as Willie and I lingered at a distance.

As we entered the waiting room, Dr. Graham said, "She's not in good condition at all. Not sure how long we can keep her body alive.

I have ordered a CAT scan of her brain to determine if there is any activity." I deeply inhaled while intensely listening to Dr. Graham's diagnosis. It was difficult trying to manage the pain of heartbreak. Dr. Graham assured us, he would return to the visitor's lounge once he received the CAT scan report. Before he exited Ebony's room, I asked, "Mom, what happened?"

In a matter of a couple of hours, the pain in my mom's eyes had added ten more years to her life. Appearing exhausted and horrified, Mom answered, "It started earlier today. Ebony was not in a good place. I noticed the last couple of days she'd been withdrawn and didn't come out of her room very much." Obviously, I contemplated whether she was telling the truth. I had spoken to Ebony a few days ago and could tell she wasn't doing well. To my recollection, Ebony had called and asked me to pick her up. Lately, Ebony and Mom hadn't been getting along. The constant strife and tension between them had escalated throughout the years. While on the phone with Ebony, she shouted, "I'm gonna kill her or myself!" I tried to assure her, "Don't worry, Ebony. Willie and I are on our way to the house." Immediately, I informed Willie what was happening. Even though my doctor had placed me on bed rest, there wasn't any question that Ebony needed me. We frantically ran out of the house and started the fifteen-minute drive to Mom's house.

With silence ringing in the car, the fifteen-minute drive felt like an hour. Entering the house, reluctantly I proceeded to say, "Mom, it may be a good idea if Ebony comes over for a couple of days. Possibly, a different environment may help." Mom was unwilling. She said, "No. And if you as much as attempt to take Ebony, I will call the police and tell them you had taken her without my permission!" Consequently, I went into Ebony's room and told her Mom's decision. I assured her everything would be alright. I told her to just keep clear of Mom for a few days, gave her a hug, and apologized again before leaving the house.

Regretfully, I never called her. Now, my mind was bombarded with countless "if's," "coulda's", and "shoulda's". "If only I would have insisted on taking her with me that day, she would still be alive." My mind was racing with endless thoughts of regret. The one person my sister trusted in the world wasn't able to save her from self-destruction. I was her older sister who had become her protector and mother figure for so many years. Ultimately, I could not protect her from herself or our mom.

My mom would never be considered for any Mother of the Year award. Her dysfunctional behavior, demanding and demeaning manner, was a bit too much to bear. It was not only unbearable for me but also Ebony. We're eight years apart, and I first experienced a mixture of emotions when Ebony was born. After being the only child for a long time, and now having a little sister, I felt a little jealous and ecstatic at the same time. Ebony was the most beautiful baby. She resembled a perfect doll: angelic, captivating and darling. Everything about her was perfect; there were no flaws.

How could Ebony be lying in the emergency room, breathless and relying on a ventilator machine to keep her alive? Within an hour, Dr. Graham returned to the visitor's waiting room with his diagnosis. Pulling the three of us together, Dr. Graham nodded his head, confirming the CAT scan report. He acknowledged there was no brain activity. In complete shock, my mom collapsed on her chair while Willie and I gazed at each other in total disbelief. Dr. Graham also informed us that Ebony had been transferred to a private room where we could now see her. Without hesitation, we hurried to the elevator that took us to her room.

No one could have prepared us for what we were about to experience. Ebony's nurse was in the room when we arrived, checking all the devices and vital signs. Underneath her soft smile, her concerned look was extremely obvious. Monitoring devices and wires were attached to Ebony for various types of observation. The constant alarming of these monitors was frightening. Sounds were coming from all the equipment. As I walked over to Ebony's bed for a closer look, bruise marks from the hair dryer cord she used for hanging remained etched around her neck. Ebony's pale skin was marred with black and blue marks.

With a painful look in her eyes, mom gave Willie and me an account of what transpired earlier that day on July 4, 2011. "Val, my downstairs neighbor, was the apartment I ran to for help. She assisted me in getting her body down from the shower, prior to the arrival of the paramedics. Ebony was totally dressed in her clothes with the shower water still running. While slobbering profusely, her voice was getting weaker and weaker with every breath she took."

My mom recalled that entire day. "Ebony had been in her room most of the day, propelling deeper into depression. I was occasionally checking on her in her room throughout the day. But this time, I noticed her looking unusually pale with eyes slightly dilated. Nearby was an empty pill bottle. Ebony began to regurgitate violently. She never said a word and never responded to any of my questions. A couple of hours later, she came from her room and informed me she was going to take a shower. Although unaware how long the water had been running exactly, I noticed it had been a while. At that time, I immediately charged the bathroom door to find her with the blow-dryer cord wrapped around her neck and attached to the shower rod. The shower water was running, and Ebony's lifeless body was dangling against the tub."

How I wanted to blurt out, "Mom, it's your fault! If only you would have let me take her with me a couple of days before this ever happened."

I had a thousand questions racing through my mind, but I couldn't articulate a single one. Too exhausted to gather any strength, I knew this was my cue to leave. I kissed my sister on her cheeks and said my goodbye to my mom. Willie and I then gathered our belongings and walked out the door.

Being surrounded by feelings that I had abandoned Ebony was overwhelming and haunting my every waking moment. Suffocating in questions of how I would move on with my life, being a mother and wife was unbearable to contemplate. Due to the excessive emotional pressure, I delivered my son eight days after my sister's suicide attempt. Al was born during the eighth month of my pregnancy. He was in a breach position, and therefore I had a C-section. I was later informed that an unborn infant has a way of securing itself in the womb when it feels an enormous amount of stress or danger. The infant feels safer tucked under a mom's ribcage, and will not move its head downward toward the birth canal.

Even an unborn child feels life's dangers. The guilt of having my son born under these adverse circumstances seemed so unfair. This wasn't how I envisioned my life. Regretfully, my mind was swimming with remorseful thoughts before I was rolled into the operating room. I was thinking, "You killed your sister. Now, you are about to kill your son." I was only twenty-one years old at the time and petrified!

Clearly, as the mother of a newborn, I wasn't mentally or physically prepared for spending long days at the hospital with my sister. My whole body felt depleted and lifeless. Ebony was hospitalized for five months. I was by her side the majority of the time. Visibly remembering myself holding my son, it somehow equated to me holding Ebony in my arms. This idea was comforting. If only there was a way for me to be transported back a couple of days before Ebony attempted suicide. I would bring her home with me, despite my mother's objections. How different our lives would be right now.

For many hours, I would stare at her, hoping somehow, by some miracle, she would open up her eyes or just move her finger, but that never happened. The body's normal reactions would cause her body to move and jerk. At first, we thought she had been given a second chance at life. The sound of the respiratory breathing almost sounded like her voice, as the air gush from the respiratory machine echoed within the room.

My mother never left her side, and signs of her deteriorating mental state were becoming more and more apparent. As I look back now, there were already signs beginning to surface months prior.

Finally, after five months of Ebony being hospitalized, the doctors assigned to her case decided it was time to hold a family meeting. We sat in a meeting room on the first floor of the hospital. Surrounded by five doctors, my mother, my husband, and I appeared terrified. We felt hopeless while waiting for them to begin the conversation. Dr. Lee was the head physician at Memorial Hospital, and he was accompanied by other doctors on the case. Dr. Graham, the emergency room doctor, was there, as well, for moral support and had been instrumental during this five-month ordeal.

Dr. Lee, displaying a melancholy look on this face, started the conversation. "Unfortunately, family, we have done all we can do." My mom gave out a heart-rending sound and placed her hands over her face, rocking back and forth uncontrollably. A few of the other doctors chimed in with their agreement. My mother was inconsolable, as she was faced with a reality that was unbearable to accept. She would never accept the fact that Ebony was brain dead, and the only reason that she was legally alive was due to the life-support machines.

The doctor further informed us that the hospital would be releasing her to a nursing facility, or she could be taken home. Unplugging Ebony from the life-support machine was not an option that my mom would ever consider.

Within a few days, she was released, and I agreed to move in with my mom to assist in Ebony's caregiving for a few months. The hospital had supplied a machine that would continue to keep my sister's organs functioning. The emotional wounds that were surfacing never diminished. So, often I would go to bed at night praying these emotional scars would miraculously be gone by the next morning. Nevertheless, my first response every morning was of extreme loss. Feelings of loss and the vulnerability that accompanied the loss caused anger. In either case, the anger helped me defend against the most painful feelings of loss by serving as a distraction.

Being a new mother and assisting with Ebony's care was exhausting. Sleepless nights and tireless days were the norm. To make matters worse, my mother was extremely manipulative and passive-aggressive. She wouldn't speak to me for days if I wanted to visit my husband late at night. I also got the "silent treatment" if I didn't accomplish things to her satisfaction.

Eventually, I took a stand and decided to no longer allow my mom control over my life, even if it meant not seeing my sister for a couple of weeks, which was usually the case. In due time, she would call and ask me if I could come and sit with Ebony while she ran some errands. I would often respond, "Sure, Mom. Of course, I will." I knew there was a possibility that weeks could pass before I would be allowed to see my sister.

The issues with my mom and I started when I was a lot younger. As a matter of fact, before Ebony was born, the dark places in my life were broad and extensive. They span back to when I was three years old. We had moved in with my uncle and his family for a season. My uncle's stepson would visit on a regular basis. The two of us, including my other cousin, would anticipate a day of games, snacks, and more playtime. It was our custom to play hide-and-seek. As kids, we always enjoyed running throughout the house, screaming and laughing. Seemingly, the louder we got, the more the fun escalated. Being that I was the youngest of us three, I always followed their lead, waiting in expectation of a fun-filled day.

During our time of hide-and-seek, my regular hiding place was in the closet belonging to my uncle and his wife. Hiding under all those clothes seemed to be the perfect place. Besides, my little body could fit snugly beneath the adult clothes without ever being detected. Well, that was my mindset at age three. However, my uncle's stepson, who was eleven years old, never had a problem finding me.

These in-house games lasted for two years, from my tender age of three to five years old. This "game" consisted of my uncle's stepson eventually finding me in my secret hiding place. Consequently, there was always a second phase of the game. Whenever I was found, he would lock the bedroom door and be completely nude. He'd also place my timid, three-year-old body on the bed before starting to molest me.

In the long run, as I grew older, telling my mom of these hideous incidents was short-lived. I was threatened if I uttered this situation to anyone. By this time, we had moved from Connecticut to Atlanta. Although months prior to my six-year-old birthday, dark, secret places of my life continued to broaden their terrible scope. During our time in Atlanta, a man, who would soon become Ebony's father, entered my mom's life. His verbal and physical abuse toward me were horrific.

He made it known to me and my mom that he didn't like me. How was I supposed to cope knowing the feelings of an adult who didn't like me, along with a mother who seemingly didn't care? The fights between them increased, comprising of him frequently lying on her and punching her in the face. On another occasion, he slammed my mom's head into a car door. All of this occurred while she was pregnant with Ebony. I witnessed everything. Confused and terrified, my eight-year-old little life had experienced a tremendous amount of trauma, yet I was unable to articulate the actions I witnessed.

Fortunately, their relationship was short-lived. Shortly after Ebony was born, he deserted his daughter and my mom. Life was becoming a horror movie with additional episodes getting worse and more intense than the previous experience. Our life had become a vicious cycle, spinning out of control with no ending in sight.

Consequently, we were on the road again. Moving from state-to-state was like traveling to the neighborhood store. Despite tears rolling down my cheeks, I was constantly uprooted from newfound friends I was finally getting to know. I couldn't fight back tears as they welled up in my eyes. Trembling after each horrendous circumstance, I was clearly upset and was feeling like a damaged little girl.

Nevertheless, I was given the job of being responsible for and assisting with the care of Ebony. I loved it! Ebony had become my escape route to peace. Dressing, feeding, and changing her diapers made me feel like her mommy. While growing up, we bonded together and became each other's rescue haven.

At the same time, our mom's deranged behavior began to surface. It was undeniably evident that our mom had severe psychological problems. One of the most remarkable features of the human mind is our incredible capacity to forget, ignore, or avoid things that worry us. We do this by means of defense mechanisms which operate unconsciously and serve to block conscious awareness of troublesome experiences and feelings. Such defense mechanisms allow us to live with pain, conflict, and trauma that are inevitably part of life. And, for this, we can be thankful. However, while these mechanisms help us cope, they also have a major negative side effect. These defense mechanisms often block growth and healing by distorting reality.

As I recall, my mom lived a life of denial, thereby creating the world which was false but real in her mind. Ebony and I were subjected to a woman, who by all accounts wasn't stable enough to raise children. Once again, my mom brought another man into our lives. She became pregnant quickly with our first brother. Within a couple of years, Mom was expecting another son. Our lives became more unmanageable in every sense of the word. Another physical abuser lived in our house. Inconceivable abuse toward me not only came from my mom, but also from her live-in boyfriend. With my mom, I was brutally beaten with rods, creating blisters on my body, whereby I could hardly sit. Her boyfriend would tell ridiculous lies to my mom about me and I would have to undress and he would beat me. It was both physically disgraceful and emotionally insulting.

Somehow, within my mother's mind, I become her enemy. She would always say, "You think you're better than me, don't you?" Yet, as I reason deep down for justification, I believe she was feeling guilty. Assuredly, the very thing she imagined was the thought she had projected onto me.

Now, let's fast-forward to the present. Surprisingly, Ebony's body managed to remain alive for three years in a comatose state. The doctors had suggested she be removed from the life-support machines on the night she was rushed to the hospital. But my mom's guilt for pushing Ebony to the edge wouldn't allow my sister to rest in peace.

For the remainder of Ebony's three years on earth, my mom moved my sister and two smaller brothers to Atlanta to be with family. I never did get a chance to say goodbye to my sister. Unexpectedly, I received a call from my mom during the afternoon. "Brea, just wanted to let you know, we have all moved to Atlanta." My mom didn't even give me the opportunity to say goodbye to my younger brothers.

After a couple of years, Ebony passed. I never received a call from my mom. My grandmother called me about Ebony's death. Although I debated whether or not to catch a flight to Atlanta, I chose against it. Too much time had already transpired between me and my mom. Going back into a battlefield with this woman was unthinkable.

Ebony had been diagnosed as bipolar with extreme manic depression. She'd been medicated and participated in therapy numerous times. Understanding her diagnosis and watching her struggle with the demons of her mental illness helped me cope with her death. This awareness also enabled me to understand why Ebony felt she had no other alternative besides suicide. Ebony's bipolar episodes were characterized by feelings of elation and high energy. However, racing thoughts, inability to sleep or even to sit still had become her nightmare. Ebony's extreme sadness and her feelings of helplessness and hopelessness were extreme.

Suicide is a scar that never heals. It removes one person's pain, while survivors often experience a lifetime of grief, guilt, and complete sadness.

Throughout the years, I've come to realize that I have nothing to defend, nothing to prove, and nothing to hide. Forgiveness toward my mom has been a walk of faith in my determination to survive this "stormy season." Dying to self has been a lifelong endeavor, even in my short-lived thirty-two years. In some ways, it feels as if I have existed on this earth a lot longer.

Emotional hurt that's bruised my heart is a result of numerous violations of trust, including a violation of my own rights. Those I trusted failed to play by the rules! Violations of trust may have been both intentional and unintentional. Despite the intention, violation of trust is an experience of hurt. Ultimately, I discovered that I'd lost much of my sense of composure, literally, I was feeling vulnerable and unhappy.

Pain associated with abandonment by a loved one, particularly a person whom one depends on for support, is probably the most powerful form of emotional abuse. Nonetheless, even when feelings of abandonment are not part of the hurtful experience, the sense of loss is overwhelming. This loss I encountered required mourning if I was to avoid becoming mentally stuck. It was my responsibility to allow the process of mourning to complete its work. Acknowledging having experienced abandonment and isolation called for resolution from within. Only then would I be able to move past hurt and anger.

The events of the last few days of Jesus' life on earth provide a good illustration. Jesus shared a final Passover meal with his disciples, despite knowing he would be betrayed and abandoned by a few of them within the next few hours. During this meal, Jesus was also confronted with discouraging evidence of how little his disciples had spiritually progressed. He heard arguments among the disciples regarding who would be considered by history as the greatest. Immediately following this meal, Jesus took them to the Garden of Gethsemane, where he asked them to wait with him while he prayed.

All of the disciples fell asleep, failing to comfort him in his hours of deep agony. He woke them, asking them to pray with him. Instead, they fell asleep once again. Quickly on the heels of this circumstance, Jesus was betrayed by Judas, abandoned by Peter, arrested, beaten, mocked, and crucified. Disheartening actions led up to his agonizing cry from the cross, "My God, my God! Why have you forsaken me?"

From being sexually abused by my uncle's stepson to the physical predators of my mom's numerous boyfriends and babies' daddies, such devastating experiences have produced a painful life. Such tragedies can never be erased from my soul. The guilt of my sister's death is etched on my heart, increasingly leaking out of my soul more and more each day. Frequently, I ask myself, "Why had they all abandoned, beaten, and emotionally crucified me?"

I've lived with unbearable scenes in my mind. But, thank God they have become a distant image, fading away as the years transpire. The Love of God has sustained me, His grace has covered me, and His forgiveness toward me has equipped me to forgive those who have hurt me.

Bruised, but not broken ...

Self-Reflection
Chapter 5

1. What pain from the past is bogging you down? What is blocking you from letting go? Is it confusing thoughts? Overwhelming feelings? Indecision?

2. What fears keep you from taking the necessary risks to move forward? What is one specific risk you can take today to begin moving forward?

3. Deuteronomy 30:19 reveals God's heart for each one of us. "Oh, that you would choose life" (*New Living Translation*). What does this mean to you? What can you do today that symbolizes you are choosing life?

Chapter 6

SEEING CLEARLY

Walking home from school in Compton, California, every day was like walking through a horrific war zone. Although I could never be certain where the attack would be deployed, I assuredly recognized I was the intended target for gang initiation. Daily, my main focus after school was getting home safely. However, I didn't have the typical peaceful views after school. My walk home consisted of an array of disturbing sights: flashing gang signs, along with witnessing people being beaten up and initiated into the gang life. I will never forget one particular occasion where a young girl, approximately 13 years old, was getting initiated into a gang. They surrounded her like vultures on the attack for their next prey. Suddenly, she was brutally punched in the face.

The girl fell but managed to get back up. As soon as she stood, another blow sent her stumbling back down. While looking on from a distance, fear gripped my heart. I wondered, "Are they going to kill her?" Unexpectedly, with eyes nearly closed, blood flowing from her swollen face, knees trembling, and looking disoriented, she was back on her feet again. It was like watching scenes from a *Rocky* movie. Over and over, she was repeatedly knocked down after rising a few more times.

Following the torturous beating, everyone was gazing at her. Finally, the leader shook her hand, uttered some words, and the other gang members embraced her like loving family members. She was being "warmly" welcomed into the ruthless gang life.

On my way home, drunken guys were frequently standing outside homes. I'd hear them yelling, "Hey, baby! Where you going?" The neighborhood was run-down with decrepit apartment buildings. You'd see broken elevators, creaky stairs, and unhinged windows that didn't fully close. Used drug needles, broken liquor bottles, and cigarette buds littered the streets. Young children sitting on apartment steps appeared as if they hadn't bathed. Time and again, I was appalled by the sight of mothers sipping beer and dragging on cigarettes, while braiding their daughters' hair. These parents were promoting ignorance as a value, and the kids in the neighborhood were naively indoctrinated into this value set. Unfortunately, the cycle repeats itself for generations.

Many of us remain in a circle of chaos when our minds keep us in an unhealthy pattern of thinking that keeps our lives in a cycle of repeating the same outcome.

What you know affects the quality of life you live, and it affects your future and your performance in life.

Generations have been hypnotized to some degree either by ideas they have accepted from others or ideas they have convinced themselves are true. These ideas can paralyze a person to a point where they can't fathom doing or being anything different from their childhood environment. You and I have been taught and trained all our lives to respond in certain ways to particular circumstances. Our hidden training comes out under pressure. Therefore, when a difficult situation occurs, your training takes over.

Once a person believes that something is true, he then acts as if it were. He will instinctively seek to collect facts to support that belief, no matter how false it may be.

There was something inside me, despite my surroundings, that desired more from life than what I had experienced. I had a gut instinct that my current options were far less than what I deserved. Perhaps, life was drawing me to a higher purpose. But fear of the future was lingering in my mind like one would feel after a nightmare. Feeling shaken to my core, the emotional chaos that flooded my soul felt like free-falling without a parachute.

But I was sincere about changing my life.

In order for me to construct a new functional building on a site where a nonfunctional building existed, I first had to raze the old structure. This was painful work, but it was done by shattering those "mistaken certainties" which prevented me from expressing the wholesome life I desired.

Everything that is built has a blueprint or plan. Each one of us has been assigned various DNA from our parents. Those genes give voice to who we are, how we respond, how we perceive, calculate, and reason. Our personalities usually coincide with our temperaments.

Our environment shapes our perception of how life should appear. Here is where our core belief system is formed. Values, judgments, habits, and religious convictions are formed at this stage of growth. It's amazing how children are molded based on their environment.

They may experience poverty, sexual or emotional abuse, and other difficult circumstances, yet they adapt and go into survival mode.

Words I constantly hear every day, or have heard that have a lasting impression on my mind, inevitably linger on in my life. Words act as a director of a movie scene or a play. Words begin to give direction to the scenes of my life.

I was determined not to allow my surroundings to imprison me and deny me access to my dreams.

While growing up in this tough neighborhood, Monica and a few of my other friends loved playing in the abandoned house on my block. The grim and gloomy house was the worst excuse for a house I'd ever seen. It was more like a long-abandoned prison or insane asylum rather than a once-nice house. The doors and windows were covered with a thick layer of dust that looked like it had been untouched for years. The door creaked open, moving open a centimeter at a time. It could move faster, but the wood of the door had grown moldy and soft with water and neglect, and if you pushed it harder, you'd probably push right through the door. It was hard to tell the original color of the carpet. Most likely, it was once beige, but now it was closer to brown. The windows were boarded up by the family who thought they would return. My mom told me it had been abandoned for years.

A house once loved, now abandoned.

In our childlike minds, we would imagine how our life would be growing up in our own house. If this is what we had to look forward to, we hadn't much anticipation for the future.

Unfortunately, my house wasn't considered a peaceful castle. It had safety bars over the windows and doors, so you get the picture. It was a small house, with three bedrooms, one bathroom, a tidy kitchen, and a moderate-sized living and dining room area. My sister and I rarely went clothes shopping, and if we did it was when JCPenney™ was having a back-to-school sale. I had one "big" birthday party. That was in the fourth grade. Most of the other years, my mom just drew a "Happy Birthday" sign and hung it in the hallway of the house. Sometimes, when things were really tight, my mom would wrap up one of my sister's current toys and give that to me as a present. I owned one bike my whole life until I left for college – a used, black, no-speed, rusted bike.

My dad was a drug dealer, therefore, it wasn't a coincidence that our house would be full of daily visitors. However, later on, I realized they were his customers, coming to fill their orders for "pharmaceutical businesses."

But I made it out–survived is more like it, because there were many things that transpired to set me up to live in this type of environment. I could have become a teenage mom. That was the norm in my neighborhood.

"Girl, have you heard that Ms. Mattie's daughter is pregnant?" "Shut your mouth, who's the daddy?" "Who knows? She's a hot mess! One day she's with Lucille's son, and the next day there's somebody else." Neighborhood gossipers had a field day with this hot topic. It was a regular occurrence to overhear similar conversations.

Girls in my neighborhood who appeared attractive to the guys had big butts, wide hips, small waists, shapely legs, and full breasts. But, those same girls didn't know the difference between a noun and a pronoun. Only one of the above character traits fit my profile.

Education was always valued high — regardless of how I "ranked" compared to other girls.

Life is about how you play the hand you're dealt. Of course, starting with a good hand of cards helps, but it doesn't determine how much you'll win or even if you'll survive the game. There are lots of people born in the worst of neighborhoods every year. Most continue the cycle and don't make it out. On top of the physical dangers you have to navigate, you also have to undo lots of damaging programming. A few folks do a little better, but their struggle continues, and they still have ties to the neighborhood. Then, there are others who escape so far from the ghetto that the experience becomes a distant memory. Such people press on to make massive changes. I can proudly say that I am part of this last group.

Despite my dad's drug dealing lifestyle, he was highly intelligent. Dad always said, "I could be anything I want to be." Oftentimes, I wondered, "How could someone be so intelligent and yet be so incapable of navigating his own life?" Inevitably, I believed him. Therefore, whatever you believe with conviction becomes your reality. You always act in a manner consistent with your deepest and most intensely held beliefs, whether they are true or not. And all your beliefs are learned. At one time, you did not have a value system. Fortunately, we are all born with a clean canvas, and we decide the picture that we create for our own life. Even with a broken crayon, you can still color your picture and design your own world.

Your beliefs largely determine your reality. You do not believe what you see. Rather, you see what you already believe. You can have life-enhancing beliefs that make you happy and optimistic, or you can have negative beliefs about yourself and your potential that act as roadblocks to the realization of everything that is truly possible for you.

Regardless of my dad's shortcomings, inability to find his own strength, and lack of courage to stand strong when the waves were crashing down, he instilled within me a few values. I learned if you believe you're limited in any area, that perception will become your truth. Dad taught that it's impossible to outperform your self-image, however, it's always possible to change and improve the image of yourself. These life lessons from my dad have become valuable tools that caused me to shift my life. In addition, my God-consciousness even in my teen years had become my safety net.

I've come to realize that transformation begins with the mind. There must be a change of thought in order to have a change of heart. And your thought life is the lens you use for visualizing and seeing things clearly. Thoughts are like prescription glasses—they give you a certain view or perspective. The lens used for vision determines your perspective. Moreover, you must have a proper perspective to make proper choices.

Speaking of making choices, I recall the time one of my friends invited me to a house party. I was sixteen at the time and eager for fun, so I accepted the invitation. Little did I realize this would be one of the turning points in my life. While putting on my party outfit, I was rehearsing in my mind the songs that I would dance to and perhaps the guys who would ask me to dance. I could hardly wait for the party.

It was time to go, and I was gathering my things. Mom was sitting on the back porch, relaxing with her feet propped on an ottoman, sipping coffee and catching up on the newspaper. She heard the porch door slam and looked up, surprised. "Mom, it's time to go," I uttered. "Go where?" she asked.

"The party is starting soon," I anxiously said. "Jackie Lynn!" Mom shouted with an extremely disgusted look on her face.

She bombarded me with a thousand questions. "Who's giving the party? Are their parents going to be there? How do you know these people?" Mom shot questions out of her mouth like sharpshooter bullets – without allowing me time to respond.

Mom reluctantly gathered her purse and keys, then stormed out the door.

She dropped Monica and me off at the house party. Monica and I grew up in the same neighborhood and had been friends since elementary school. She liked the same type of music, and on occasion had a crush on the same guy. Considering Monica's eagerness for a fashionable outfit, you would have thought we were going to our senior prom party. With much deliberation, Monica and I decided we would wear the same color outfit. A stylish purple skirt and black blouse was what we agreed upon, after much dispute. Somehow, she always had the upper hand. She was overbearing – her ideas seemingly superseded anything I had to offer. I was soft-mannered and accommodating. It was less stressful than to argue any facts.

The party was only a few blocks away, but it felt like we were never going to arrive.

Overly anxious to get inside, we barely said our goodbyes to Mom as we exited the car.

"You girls call me when you're ready for me to pick you up," my mom exclaimed, calling out in a high voice. "Alright mom," I replied without looking back at her.

The house party was jam-packed and hot. The crowd was so dense and loud that Monica and I could hardly hear each other. Shoving our way through the crowd shoulder-to-shoulder was irritating, when searching for the dance floor. After finally approaching the dance floor, we were too exhausted to dance. To my surprise, we locked eyes with a few of our friends. Monica and I exhaled a sigh of relief. We knew the night would be fun.

It appeared to be two parties inside of one house: a disaster waiting to happen. There was an assortment of inappropriate activities: underage drinking, drugs, smoking, drinking games, flirting, and displays of manliness. But another group was more civilized and tame. We chose the latter group for our association.

Within a few minutes, this guy came towards us. He was big-shouldered in a fashionably-ripped black T-shirt, with a massive chest. In a husky voice, he asked me to dance.

"Sure, why not?" I replied. Looking back at Monica, I searched her face for approval as we entered the dance floor. She had an uncharacteristically cruel smile ease across her face. However, Monica gave me a "thumbs up" simultaneously. Her contagious laughter made the night even more fun.

The night was everything we thought it would be and even more. We both danced throughout the evening, told jokes, embarrassed ourselves, and made lots of new friends, until all of a sudden, we realized it was time to call my mom. The party was ending in about

15 minutes. I borrowed the house phone to call Mom and inform her the party was ending. After answering the phone on the first ring, she blurted out, "I'm on my way."

Making our way through the crowd to the door was less strenuous since we were all heading in the same direction. We finally made it to the door and down the steps to the yard after smiling and waving goodbye to our friends.

Suddenly, we heard these loud pops. We didn't know where they originated and first thought we were hearing firecrackers. Everyone started running in sheer fear and terror, seeking cover behind each other and parked cars. Someone next to me looked at me and shouted, "She's been shot in the eye!" My shirt was soaking with blood. Collapsing to the ground, I noticed a guy lying nearby on the ground. He was about 12-feet away and surrounded in a puddle of blood. I later discovered he was killed by the bullets that I assumed were firecrackers.

Quickly, I began experiencing a multitude of symptoms. Chills ran up my spine. I was sweating profusely. All I could think about was my future; would I live to have one? I had just become another statistic – an innocent victim of a drive-by shooting! Although this night started out fun, it quickly turned disastrous.

Within minutes of the shooting, I arrived at UCLA-Harvard Hospital – a giant, sterile maze on the border of northwest and northeast Los Angeles. Here, doctors treat so many victims of violent crime that the government sends their military surgeons here before deploying them into battle zones, or so I was later told.

After waking up in the emergency room, I didn't know if I would live or die. The nurse informed me I had also been shot in the shoulder as well. They cut my blouse and realized it had masked a badly hemorrhaging shoulder wound. My adrenaline-fueled defiance gave way to the gory injury staring me in the face. I had an epiphany: I'd been shot, but I'm alive.

The trauma doctors immediately rushed me into surgery. I woke up a few hours later in recovery. My family members were there. Although I was extremely groggy and wearing an oxygen mask, I knew where I was and why. I wiggled my shoulder. "Feels fine," I thought to myself.

The hospital nurse placing a bedpan under me said, "You need to buy a lottery ticket. That's how lucky you were!" Apparently, the bullet barely missed my eye, grazing my eyelid, but the gun fragments were still lodged in my eye. I flinched when the pain started to surface. Pain medication would suffice for only a few hours. They ran fluids into a vein in my left arm to revive dropping blood pressure. I no longer felt like I was on the verge of unconsciousness, but for the first time, I could feel the full extent of the pain wracking my upper body.

I spent a week in the hospital, but never without company. When the hospital released me, I was in good shape physically. However, I required much healing mentally and emotionally. I made a vow to myself: I wouldn't let what happened to me change the way I approach life.

At that moment, I knew that I didn't live under a glass ceiling, and there was nothing impossible to achieve. In only a matter of months, surgeons carefully removed the bullet fragments from my eye, and I was able to graduate the following year on time.

This was an exceptionally dark chapter in my life. Nonetheless, it's not the complete book.

My last year in high school was nothing I had imagined. Memories of the shooting lingered in the back of my mind similar to the effects of an explosion that carries shock waves. I began experiencing post-traumatic stress disorder.

Walking to the neighborhood store or to school started off as a pleasant and invigorating experience. Flashbacks of crowds toppling over others while running from the bullets eroded my mind. My heart would quickly palpitate. I could feel the pulse in my throat while gasping for air. One flashback would have me breathing heavily, perspiring, and would cause overall body tension.

Resounding chatter in the back of my mind was ever-present. "Did the guy who shot me see me? Was he coming after me? Why me?" Day-after-day, I was being paralyzed, reliving that night as if it had just occurred. Once again, fear had its clutches on me.

Perspective determines how you see life's situations. In life, there is no option for failure. There is either winning or learning.

That day, I chose not to wear the victim mentality lens of self-pity. Nor did I wear the martyr mentality lens, thinking I was the only one experiencing this type of crisis. The condemned mentality lens was not welcome: discounting myself and refusing to believe I deserve the best. Finally, the unworthy mentality lens had to be evicted: lacking value, worthless, undeserving. I chose to wear the sonship mentality lens: "I am a child of God, and He has the last say over my life."

When I graduated from high school, it was liberating. In my mind, residing in the same community kept me bound to my environment. It had become a constant reminder of defeat and tragedy. Even though a year had passed, tragedy remained in my present condition.

I had reached an intersection I needed to cross in order to arrive at another point of purpose. Strategies and systematic approaches were incorporated into my life. The time had come for me to attend college. I was the first college student in my family, and everyone was ecstatic.

To make ends meet, I worked part-time while attending college. I had a slew of odd jobs. I worked at a halfway house, as a hair braiding stylist, a Macy's salesperson, and an airport security guard. With such jobs, I was able to provide for my minimal lifestyle. The city bus and my legs were my means of transportation. Despite my financial hardship, my grades were never affected. On countless days, I didn't have enough food to eat, but God brought someone across my path who would offer to buy me a meal.

My human angel was in the person of Ms. Nancy, my landlord. She offered me the opportunity to clean her house in exchange for a portion of my rent when I was short on money. It was during these times that my faith grew. Faith lies on the other side of logic. Faith is what makes life bearable, with all its tragedies and fears.

Have you ever watched a small child transition from an infantile state of total dependence to relative independence? As he learns life skills like dressing, brushing teeth, and combing hair, he develops a confident attitude. He declares, "I can do it myself!" This attitude, encouraged by parents and reinforced by a culture that prides itself on its own resourcefulness, can become a stronghold of self-reliance. And self-reliance shuts out God.

I learned this truth the hard way. I had always been an independent person. Though I was quick to seek God's intervention in circumstances that were beyond my control, I tried to handle the bulk of life's situations on my own. In fact, I thought that God wanted me to be self-reliant.

But as I grew closer to God, I learned I was wrong. I began to pray, "Lord, show me anything that is a hindrance to knowing You." One day, when I uttered this prayer in the presence of God, He filled my room. I came to understand that He didn't want me to wait until I had run out of my own resources to put things into His hands. He wanted me to depend on Him for everything!

Total dependence on God is not weakness. It is a place of surrender that acknowledges we can do nothing without Him. We can take this stance in confidence, knowing that whatever resources we need, He will provide, and whatever tasks He assigns, He will do through us.

It was my total dependence on God that gave me the strength to graduate from California State University Los Angeles with a bachelor's degree in management, and two master's degrees: a Master of Health Administration and Master of Business Administration.

But the father who instilled in me the knowledge that I could do anything, died in an ICU unit from sclerosis of the liver in 2006. Dad's addictions would not allow him to live what he taught. He wasn't able to bounce back from life's disappointments, devastations, and difficulties. These dilemmas spilled over into every facet of his life, de-fueling his opportunities and possibilities.

Dad was diagnosed with sclerosis of the liver several years prior to his death, and it took a horrendous toll on his health. Since then, my father had become more of an alcoholic than ever. He hadn't seen a doctor in over a year and had no desire. He was looking more sickly every day, with liver spots all over his face, noticeable weight loss, and swelling in his stomach and legs. His mental behavior had also worsened; he began experiencing memory loss and had spider veins all over his body. Seeing my father in this terrible physical condition was difficult to handle.

My hopes of hearing him say he was proud of my accomplishments were dashed. Dad was the one man constantly reminding me of my greatness while refusing to walk in his own greatness. Consequently, he was unable to bounce back from his internal struggle and rather became a passive recipient of what life served him.

Sometimes, when you've struggled, you think that the struggle is just a way of life. You adjust to the perspective, which is contrary to God's will for your life. We look at other people and think that God could not possibly do for you what he has done for them. Oftentimes, after living a long life of degradation, many give up too soon. However, the power of the Holy Spirit whispers into your being, "Get up!" Then, it empowers you to face the next challenge.

Do you have the strength to survive on the whisper of the Holy Spirit? He whispers into your soul, but if you magnify the wrong voice, the real voice will not be heard. There is a champion in you, but champions endure all obstacles because they have learned to listen to the whisper of the Holy Spirit.

As I began to liberate myself through God's Word, I no longer saw myself as a disempowered victim of circumstance. I learned to live from inside out, to make right choices, and to see that I could take responsibility for my life conditions. With the mindset of a survivor instead of a victim, I surrendered to situations over which I had no control. I moved out of my life what I did not want and made room for what I desired. As a result, my whole life changed from the inside-out.

Bruised, but not broken...

Self-Reflection
Chapter 6

1. Healing requires patience. What do you tell yourself that keeps you from being able to relax when things don't go according to your timetable?

2. What are three unrealistic expectations you have about things in your life? How do these set you up for disappointment?

3. Life becomes sweeter as we enthusiastically embrace our future. For which of the following things do you need to ask God to help you embrace your future: wisdom, strength, confidence, friendships, protection, courage, forgiveness, hope?

Chapter 7

UNCONDITIONAL LOVE

My parents, Ron and Jackie Smith, were anxiously waiting for the call from the adoption agency to inform them of my birth. They were on pins and needles in anticipation of this phone call. Unfortunately, Mom wasn't able to conceive. Mom and Dad's ultimate desire was to have their own children. Seven years earlier, they adopted my brother Anthony, yet their void wasn't quite fulfilled. With a great deal of love to give and spread around, my parents decided to adopt again. Brenda was added to the growing family.

After another seven years had passed, my parents decided once more to adopt. On February 9, 1967, the Smiths received their long-awaited call regarding my birth. Two days later, the couple picked me up from the hospital. I was happily added to our loving family. And boy, am I grateful!

My mother told me of an incident that happened when I was only one. We were in a horrible accident. Mom painfully articulated how she climbed into the back of the ambulance with my grandmother and me to sit at our side. She tightly held my grandmother's hand with her right hand and held mine with her left. Mom was struggling to do all of this while rolling next to the stretcher. She couldn't muster a sound, so she kept tightly clenching our hands. Mom was exhausted. She was suffering from a fractured arm and couldn't verbalize her immense pain.

Inside the ambulance, Mom was seated next to the paramedic technician. She was quietly frantic. "How could this be happening?" she finally mustered the energy to whisper. Usually strong and fearless, yet nurturing, Mom couldn't manage to hide the tears softly falling onto the sheets. With a wipe of a tear and a long, loud sigh, she repeated again, "How could this be happening?"

Grandmother was unconscious and required life-saving treatment. The paramedics immediately began performing cardiac support, providing emergency respiratory procedures, and administering intravenous fluids to my grandmother.

The paramedics assumed my condition was less life-threatening based on the horrific screams echoing through the ambulance. Upon arriving at the hospital, the policeman who was on the scene introduced himself as Sergeant Jones. By this time, my mom was seated in a wheelchair. My grandmother and myself were taken to separate rooms. As mom recounted the story, it was as if she was reliving the horrific event. "All I could recall was the heavy rain, a car crashing in front of me, a big flash of light, then a jerk," she said. Taking in another huge breath, Mom continued, "The next thing I knew, I was hearing squealing tires, breaking glass, and feeling the car flipping over." Emotionally traumatized over this tragedy, Mom shut her eyes tightly and inhaled deeply. She took a moment and whispered, "Then, everything went silent."

The next moments are the most painful for Mom. An emergency physician approached, informing Mom that I had a broken pelvic bone and was being prepped for surgery. With a reassuring look in his eyes, he said, "But, she is expected to recover. Unfortunately, were unable to save your mother."

Mom lost her composure, completely breaking down in her wheelchair. Quivering, feeling weightless, and crying, she uttered, "If only I wouldn't have picked her up in all this rain. She would still be with us. She needed a few items from the supermarket."

Consequently, another car was involved in the accident. Due to the heavy rainstorm, both drivers were blinded by the weather. The cars came around a sharp curve from opposite directions. While attempting to avoid each other, both vehicles lost control on the slippery road. Sliding into the other car was unavoidable. Unfortunately, our car was sideswiped and experienced the most damage. The couple driving the other vehicle managed to escape with only minor injuries.

My mom later told me of this terrible accident shortly before I entered first grade. I was experiencing periodic pain in my lower abdomen due to the accident. It was a regular occurrence to visit the doctor bi-annually for exams. The practitioners wanted to ensure that the artificial pelvic bone was intact and adapting to my growth. Sadly, during this time, the doctor also informed my parents it was not likely that my artificial pelvis could accommodate the birthing of a child the conventional way.

Despite this prognosis, growing up as a six year old and playing "dress up" in my mother's clothes in order to feel like a Hollywood movie star was thrilling. Wearing oversized high heels and a dress with a waistline reaching my toes, always sent me daydreaming of wearing glamorous adult clothes. I can count the years spent "playing house" and pretending to be a mom I never knew. However, I never imagined my childhood would end so abruptly.

I still remember arguing with Mom and Dad because I was not allowed to cross the street alone. I thought that was a "little kid" rule. Now, I wish I could have the simple rules back. I'd love to drain the last bit of being a kid out of my life before moving on to harsher rules in a much more ruthless world.

By the time I was in elementary school, my parents told me they had adopted me from infancy. It didn't seem worth mentioning. But hot off the press, I eagerly told my classmate the very next day. I happily said to her, "I'm adopted!" "No, you're not," she replied. "You're lying." I was hurt. "I really am," I said, bursting into tears. I told the teacher's aide, and within minutes I was already over it. But, the aide apparently saw the chance for a teachable moment.

"Do you know why you were adopted?" she asked. I told her it was because when I was a baby, my biological mother didn't want to take care of me anymore. "Didn't want to, or couldn't?" she asked pointedly. Honestly, I didn't know and hadn't thought about it when I first found out. Quite naturally, when asked by the aide, I was taken aback. I answered, "I guess it was because she couldn't," though the distinction hardly seemed important.

Who cared if she could or couldn't, didn't want to or simply didn't care? I was a happy, smart child who insisted on wearing only dresses to school and who commanded the room with my bubbly personality.

I was delightful. As far as I was concerned, if this mysterious woman didn't want me, it was her loss.

Growing up in our family was similar to any other family. Sibling rivalry, house cleaning chores, misbehavior issues, attitudes displayed from time-to-time were all part of the childhood experience. We "did life" together, despite the growing pains. Nevertheless, our home environment was nurturing, yet strict. Our parents were church-going folks, and an "absent pass" from Sunday's service was not easily given. Unfortunately, you were expected to have at least a 101° body temperature, been up all night with diarrhea, or up all night regurgitating. Otherwise, the church was your destination early Sunday morning.

We attended the Baptist church near our home. My parents actually grew up in that church, and so did their parents. Like clockwork, at ten-thirty on a Sunday morning, we would be pulling up in the parking lot of Saint Matthew's Baptist Church, all three kids tucked neatly in the back seat of the car. Dressed in our Sunday's best, afraid to get too close together, in fear that our freshly-starched clothes would possibly become wrinkled.

As we entered the church building, one of the ushers would kindly greet us. It was like he pushed a "playback" button every Sunday. I always wondered where his tape recorder was located. I'd silently answer myself, "It must be in his jacket pocket." The black suit he wore every Sunday was shiny with stripes, and his white shirt stood out very prominently. But one thing was different, he switched ties every Sunday. His black patent leather shoes were always shiny – like they'd been recently polished. In his raspy voice, he would say, "Well good morning, family. How is everyone doing this fine Sunday morning?" Mom or Dad would reply, "All is well. Thank you for asking."

We weren't allowed to sit in the back seat of the church with the other kids. Everyone was aware that kids kept themselves occupied during service by passing notes, drawing pictures, or throwing spitballs from the back of the row at each other. However, on one particular Sunday, one of the spitballs missed the intended target and hit a congregant in the back of the neck.

Like a domino effect, all the kids put their heads down, trying to avoid eye contact with Miss Scott as she quickly turned around. Without hesitation, she immediately got up and stormed to the back few rows where the kids were sitting, asking, "Who threw that spitball?" Everyone, in unison, replied, "Not me." In a stern voice, Miss Scott said, "Well, somebody did it! It just didn't throw itself." Her glaring eyes made contact with everyone in those two rows. She headed back to her seat. While crossing over other congregants, Miss Scott occasionally looked back at us. If eyes could kill, we would all be laid out.

On our way home from church, we knew our parents had gotten wind of the report. So, we weren't thrilled to be back in the car. Mom had always been the disciplinarian. Before we could exit the parking lot, Mom spoke in a thunderous tone. "I got news today that one of the kids threw a spitball and accidentally hit Miss Scott on the back of her neck." All three of us straightened our posture and sat glued to the rear seat of the car, appearing worried. None of us kids uttered a sound.

Ordinarily, my brother Anthony would be the one to intervene and tell his side of the story. Being that he was a lot older than me and my sister. But not this time. Unexpectedly leaning forward, with my voice cracking, I said, "It was me." For the first twenty seconds, the car was silent. Surprisingly, my dad bellowed out, "You know that behavior isn't tolerated, young lady!"

"Yes, sir, I replied," looking down. I was afraid he would turn his head away at any time.

Disappointing my father was the worst thing I could ever imagine. He looked straight ahead, but it was like his eyes were in the back of his head, glaring at me. "Daughter," he would call me when trouble was brewing in the Smith house, "Punishment is in order! Starting today, no playtime for you—not today or after school for one week!" This meant from the time I got home from school, my bedroom was my prison until the next morning.

Frequent bathroom visits were always an excuse to escape the boredom of the four walls. It felt like a prison sentence without bars. Instead, my bedroom door kept me ostracized from the rest of the house. I also lost the privilege of enjoying family time. When punishment was finally lifted, you could only find me in my bedroom during bedtime. As an extremely talkative person, punishment was mental torture.

Growing up a teenager entailed a great deal of responsibility and I encountered situations I would never have dreamed of experiencing as a young child. I based my life on TV, believing a teenager's life consisted of dealing with zits, who wore the latest fashions or dated which boyfriend that week. But, as I grew into my teen years, it was apparent that TV doesn't always show what is actually coming in real life.

The effects of being adopted began to surface. Unfortunately, feelings of not knowing my other family "out there," including siblings or extended family members, started to harness my mind. Simultaneously, the thought of leaving the adoption as a "done deal," moving on and releasing the past created constant mental warfare.

Regardless of mental turmoil clouding my mind, there was always a sense of security and peace around me.

Mom was a devout woman of prayer who instilled within me this same fervent prayer life. In fact, our house became a house of prayer for the neighborhood children. Her stories of answered prayers always entertained us, as we sat at her feet, glued to each detail. Oftentimes, while gazing at Mom in amazement, she would tell the same story. However, each re-telling always sounded completely different from the last narrative.

Mom had experienced God. Her narratives were filled with treasure and substance.

It was those stories that anchored me during my "dumb teen days" and even into adulthood.

I met the love of my life at 19 in what seemed like a romance that couldn't go wrong. I said, "Yes," to his proposal, and we were married shortly thereafter. It had all the bells and whistles that guaranteed a life of bliss. Unbeknownst to me, the warm fuzzy feeling was not an indication of true love and was short-lived. Here I was, living with a momma's boy, who failed to grow up. When the signs of immaturity were shown, I missed the cues. Giving the silent treatment during an argument, changing jobs regularly, incessantly playing video games, along with speeding and racing other cars at stoplights are a short list of his juvenile behavior.

Here I was expecting someone with 24-ounces of love to fill a 64-ounce cup. Sadly, I was unaware my expectations of him were unrealistic. He was only able to love me to the capacity he was able to love himself. Unconsciously, I was starting to carry around an "excuse bag." This bag was filled with excuses like, "He really loves me, but he doesn't know how to show it." "He's really a nice guy, he just needs some help learning how to express his emotions." Besides, I believed marriage was made to be forever.

Our relationship was void of three healthy important ingredients. First, reciprocity, where both people are equally invested in the relationship. Second, generativity, because our relationship never experienced a new understanding, a new solution with each encounter. Thus, it never moved forward and remained stagnant. Third, honesty, whereas, I was never able to feel free to tell him what was on my mind, and trying to gauge his response by revealing his true thoughts, motivations, and intentions. Thus, we were continually never getting to know each other better. So, here we were – stuck, not having the understanding of how to get un-stuck. Somehow, we failed to realize that we were dealing with our own excuse bags and our own junk in our trunk.

It's a red flag if you have to call your friends or obtain a Ph.D. to decipher what your mate is trying to communicate to you. For example, you think you are having engaging discussions, but you walk away feeling confused after each conversation. Or, you worry about whether he's telling you the truth. Many times, you try to communicate with him, but he hears a message other than what you said. Eventually, you realize that if you cannot communicate about the simplest of things, you might not be able to build a solid relationship together.

Is there one relationship problem that eats away at you, but you don't know why? You keep trying to connect the dots, but you can't, and you wonder if there's a deeper issue that you are missing? Or, whether the problem is serious enough to be considered a deal breaker?

I soon realized that a deal breaker is not a one-time fight. Nor is it an excuse to put distance between you and him. A deal breaker is a sign of everything that is wrong in a relationship. As I started exploring our issues, it became obvious that sometimes deal breakers erupt into consciousness. During one awful moment, I discovered a pile of bounced checks after it was long-suspected that my husband was irresponsible. Deal breakers can also be characterized by a series of minor events that add up to one big problem. For example, on numerous occasions, I caught my husband inappropriately looking at other women.

True deal breakers are symptomatic of underlying relationship problems. They point to something severe, such as a relationship impasse or a destructive emotional issue that cannot be resolved. As such, deal breakers become signposts of other dynamics that are unworkable in a relationship.

The "deal breaker" sign was no longer in my side view – it was right in front of me. The signs soon became a turning point for me. Although I was not ready to give up my excuse bag completely, at least the realization of them began to surface. My husband's controlling and manipulative behavior became undeniable. It was apparent that I had possibly made a mistake in marrying him.

And then, unexpectedly becoming pregnant at twenty-one was not the most favorable thing to do. Yet, when I found out, I was thrilled. Once I knew I was pregnant, watching out for my life in a bigger way became more necessary. The same problems with my husband kept resurfacing, but my focus was on the bigger picture: giving birth to a healthy child. Despite the marital conflict, my unborn child was the most important thing.

I remember being eight months pregnant, returning home from the supermarket carrying a bag full of groceries. While huffing and puffing, the phone rang. Although nearly tripping over the grocery bag that was situated on the floor, I reached over to the phone that was positioned on the wall.

I was visually upset, saying to myself, "Who is calling now?" On the other side of the phone, it was my mom. Sensing a little disturbance in her voice, she said, "I just received a call from the adoption agency. Your biological mother contacted them and was hoping you would be open to meeting her." Holding the phone was excruciating. I nearly dropped the bag already slipping from my arms. For now, managing to gently place the grocery bag on the floor and exhale a few times was all I could do for the next few seconds.

The first thing that occurred was an odd statement from Mom. "That's strange," Mom remarked, "What's strange?" Before I could answer, Mom proceeded to say, "Get a paper and pen, and write this number down. They are expecting you to call them back with an answer." I fumbled a minute while attempting to locate paper. "Alright, Mom. Let me get my thoughts together, and I'll call you later." We said our goodbyes, while simultaneously looking at the number. I knew a decision wouldn't be made today. So, I placed the number in the kitchen drawer before putting away the groceries.

I couldn't sleep. Tossing and turning all night, going over and over in my mind, "What should I do?" was part of many racing thoughts throughout the night. When the dawn of a new day was shining through my mini-blinds, I knew a decision had to be made. Picking up the phone to first inform my parents of my decision was liberating, yet stressful at the same time. Speaking out loud, "How would they feel knowing my decision to contact the adoption agency? Would they be hurt and disappointed?" Regardless of my decision, knowing how much they loved me, my heart whispered, "It will be fine." And it was. My parents only confirmed what I perceived was correct. They only wanted the best for me. Now feeling assured, I was ready to make the call. I gave a big sigh of relief after pulling the paper containing the contact information out of the drawer. Then, I made the call.

Preparing to meet my biological mother for the very first time was an extremely intimidating and stressful experience. Despite your age when this momentous experience occurs, there are many issues that must be considered when meeting your birth mother for the first time.

I was unaware of what I was looking for. Acceptance, a rational explanation as to why I was put up for adoption, I may not get those. Looking for some self-identity, possibly, that may not be available either. At any rate, finally, the day had arrived, and both my parents offered to go with me.

Fear of the unexpected overtook me while walking through the front door of the adoption agency. I was eight months pregnant, and my adopted parents were beside me. We were escorted to a meeting room with chairs and tables. Sitting there was a woman whose physical appearance resembled mine. Today was the day I would finally confront the real reason for my adoption. Consequently, I also had to personally admit my adoptive family, whom I dearly loved, did not bring me into this world. I would soon realize the nurturing and love I received from my adoptive family will never disappear just because I was meeting my birth mother "Laura."

We gently embraced; it was like meeting a stranger for the first time. However, Laura was overwhelmed with relief after finally meeting her daughter whom she had given up for adoption 21 years earlier. We sat for a few hours, having small talk, and eventually, the conversation shifted to more of a serious tone. Laura started describing my older brothers who were taken away from her at the ages of three and four years old. Details were also given about her reason for giving me up for adoption, and how she's spent these past 43 years.

Laura handed me a photo album of family members, somehow trying to play "catch-up," introducing me to all the family members I never met. When I finally had time to take it all in, I felt like the result of a mishandled science experiment. I wondered what might have happened to me if I had been raised by my genetic parents. It seems unlikely I would've ended up with the degree of ambition that I possess, one that surpasses my modest genetic gifts.

We exchanged numbers and promised to remain in contact. Periodically, we talked until the delivery of my daughter. Coincidently, I went into labor one month after meeting Laura and delivered my daughter that same day.

The following day, my biological mother visited us at the hospital. It was quite apparent she was under the influence of some substance. Laura entered my room, wide-eyed, smiling from ear-to-ear, speaking with a slur, and behaving extremely hyperactively. Looking around frantically, she asked, "Where is the baby?" Speechless, in pain, and a bit fearful, I asked myself, "What is the woman doing here?" I suddenly remembered my mom telling me earlier that morning, she had called Laura about the baby's birth. Laura went on to rehearse everything she had previously told me during our initial visit at the adoption agency.

Once again, she shared how she suddenly became aware of exactly what she needed to do. "Perhaps," Laura said, "I had been dreaming, but I felt as if I had somehow been told that adoption was the best choice for everyone involved - especially the baby." I went back to sleep that night finally feeling some sense of inner peace. It was as if that was the first time I really heard this story.

At the same time, I wondered, "What have I allowed into my world?" I was at a loss for words, but clearly thinking, "There is no connection here, except for the mere fact she was the womb that brought me into this world."

A few minutes later, the nurse came in with my daughter for her regular two-hour feeding. Despite looking surprised to see my visitor, the nurse politely greeted Laura, gave me my daughter, and exited the room. Immediately, Laura made her way to the bed, looking intensely at my daughter and then at me. I had no inclination of what she was thinking but felt like I needed to hold the baby tightly while feeding her. Perhaps, Laura was rehearsing in her own mind the day she delivered me, or she was experiencing regret.

Nevertheless, she took a seat and continued her conversation. What was to follow was never mentioned at the adoption agency. Laura informed me the staff had asked for a list of qualities she wanted prospective parents to possess. I was "matched" with three potential couples, and she was given their profiles to read. Each letter provided information about what each person did for a living, their general interests, and information about their extended families. Tearfully, Laura explained how these letters gave insight into each couple's background. After looking around the room, Laura said, "I hope I chose the right parents for you." It was as if she had sobered up to tell me that story. Returning back to her "incoherent" condition, Laura asked, "Can I have her?" Appearing amazed and confused, I replied, "You can't have my baby!" By that time, the nurse had returned to the room. Before leaving to return the baby to the nursery, the nurse informed us that visiting hours had ended. I was relieved. Laura gave me a kiss on my forehead and left.

It seemed like a matter of five minutes when the nurse returned, informing me that my mother was displaying disturbing behavior while leaving. Laura was acting unreasonable and screaming at the nurses, "I'm the real grandmother!" Eventually, they called security to escort Laura out of the hospital. I was also informed Laura was no longer allowed at the hospital.

The head nurse on-call that night filed a complaint and advised me it wasn't a good idea for Laura to return to the hospital. I immediately informed my husband and my parents of the incident, and we were all relieved that safety measures were in place. Hospital administrators decided it was best to move my room and provide a pseudonym for the remaining few days my hospital stay.

Because of her unruly behavior, my family felt it was warranted that we change our phone numbers and keep our distance. One month passed, then two and then three. We got word that my mother had died. Laura had died from a drug overdose. Apparently, she was in a hotel room in Oregon doing drugs. The person left her in the hotel and called the paramedics. The technician worked on her for some time but wasn't able to resuscitate her. The technician later informed us that Laura gave up and stopped fighting to remain alive.

My biological mother, who had birthed three children she barely knew, was now dead at the age of 44 years old. She died brokenhearted and regretful.

Laura's chemical addiction opened the door to spiritual oppression. While speaking with a friend who worked in a drug abuse clinic that treated heroin addicts, I learned about addiction. After a time, she noticed all of the patients behaved somewhat alike. It was almost as if the addiction had a personality, a pattern of behavior similar in every person. The peculiar thing was that addicts didn't live together or interact with each other, nor did they have an environment in common. They came from wealthy and poor homes, large and small families, single, and two-parent homes. In short, the most common denominator among them was drugs.

Laura, the lady whom I never got to know, never knew Jesus is intimately acquainted with our hurts, fears, and problems. He is the only one who can truly heal and lead us through the valley of the shadow of death into the pastures of emotional and mental peace. Receiving significant inner healing, I've learned without a doubt that the most important ingredient in receiving emotional healing is faith in God and His love for us.

Faith is the power and love of God and what gives us the ability to face our fears and hurts. Faith is what gives us the hope for tomorrow when our days are filled with pain and heartache. Faith in God is what gives us the ability to dream of a place of quiet waters and green pastures when we are brokenhearted and regretful. We don't have to live with guilt, regret, or shame anymore. Too many people are stuck with memories from their past they're unable to release. Either you've been hurt and have resentment, or you've hurt someone else and you have guilt.

Laura never forgave herself, even though her children received a better quality of life than she could ever provide. Unforgiveness has the power to separate us from God. It is the fuel that energizes bitterness and resentment, two forms of spiritual cancer. Once these cancers have taken root and residence in our hearts, we are vulnerable to everything from physical illness to emotional misery. Like all forms of cancer, regret and resentment spread to others. Many have been plundered and ravished by this spiritual disease. Unfortunately, unforgiveness put us in a prison of pain. Unforgiveness also has the power to blind our spiritual and mental eyes.

God doesn't want you to carry that heavy baggage throughout your life. God's Word cleanses the dirt, clears the mind, and washes our bodies. The Word releases all the dirt, junk, grime, grit, shame, and the sin out of our lives.

Time, patience, and commitment to God's principles and ways are required to change. Our Christian experience doesn't magically erase pain or consequences from the past. Instead, our faith empowers us to live life according to God's will.

My mother never had the courage to confront her issues. As a result, her children, the brothers I never met, and the granddaughter she never held, are living life without her today.

Healing the mind, body, and spirit is similar to nurturing a tree. A tree is made of three basic parts: the root, sap, and body. In caring for a tree, it is important to prune off dead branches. Yearly, it becomes necessary to spray for insects, bores, or fungus. Attending to the needs of that tree based on what lies above ground is definitely important. However, there is more. Underneath is a complex root system that sustains, nourishes, and supports the tree. The root system must be nourished as well. Without it, no amount of pruning, spraying, or medicating will completely restore a sick tree to health.

Oftentimes, we try to deal with our problems like a person attempting to heal a tree while ignoring the root system. The root system is our heart. Man cannot effectively change his behavior without also changing his heart. The unseen root system must also be treated. We aren't able to become totally free until we handle the issues of the heart.

Occasionally, my necklaces get knotted and twisted. Unfortunately, someone else has to untangle them for me. Whoever gets the job must painstakingly unravel the twisted mass. Ever so gently, they unknot the necklaces, untangle the strands, freeing them from knotted prisons, and laying each whole piece straightly on the counter.

Our lives are similar to those chains. We, too, come to our heavenly Father holding the twisted, knotted tangle of our lives, and lifting our hands up to God, we ask Him to "fix it." He reaches down and takes our knotted, hurting hearts. Although He now possesses our hearts, He does not stop there. He lays our lives out in front of Him and begins the process of untangling the issues and hurts that have besieged us for so long. Ever so gently and carefully, He frees us from our prison of pain and conflict, laying to rest each issue of our lives, straight, untangled, and unknotted. What makes Him do this for us? Because He loves us and wants to enjoy us. He also allows us to enjoy Him and each other. Personal, passionate, pure love is His motivation toward you right now and for the rest of your life.

Thankfully, the foundation of a God-centered life that my parents instilled in me remains my shelter in the midst of a storm.

Bruised, but not broken …

Self-Reflection
Chapter 7

1. When you think back over your life, which childhood loss was most painful? What helped you keep going? What did you learn from this dark time?

2. What was your family "rule" about coping with pain? (e.g., ignore it, stuff it, fake it, or express it) How does this rule affect you today?

3. Begin the process of letting go of your grief by writing down your most painful losses, then consider doing one of the following: burn your paper in the fireplace, shred your paper, or wrap your paper around a rock and throw it into a lake, river, or ocean.

ABOUT THE AUTHOR

Linda G. Hodge is a wife, mother, grandmother, author, and eloquent motivational speaker. Linda also co-pastors with her husband of 35- plus years, Dr. Fred L. Hodge, Jr. at Living Praise Christian Center in Chatsworth and Palmdale, California. They have five children and eight grandchildren. She is a successful entrepreneur, author, and conference speaker. Linda has created and produced conferences, seminars, and extreme makeovers designed to equip, support, and empower women to live in their divine destiny. She has presently authored five books: ***Woman Under Construction, Woman Under Construction Tool Book, Winning In Life: How to Bounce Back from Adversity, 52 Questions and Answers for Singles*** and a new release, ***Bruised but Not Broken: From Private Pain to Public Victory.***

Linda and her husband are founders of Transformation Mentoring, which consists of workshops that dig deep into the soul to root out false beliefs and self-sabotaging behaviors so that a person is repositioned to move forward in their dreams and desires. She is a certified life coach assisting women in breaking free from procrastination by identifying roadblocks and negative thought patterns. Linda helps women see possibilities in their lives by setting goals and organizing their priorities. She guides them to develop their strengths so that they can live the productive life they deserve. Linda and her husband can be heard on their weekly podcast, **Winning In Life**.

Linda has a personal testimony that God has a restoration plan for all those who have been broken, hurt, displaced, or abused. She is a firm believer that what is within you is greater than anything that is in your surroundings.

You can follow Linda on Facebook, wovenwomennetwork.net, and LindaGHodge.com

Linda G. Hodge, Author
www.transformationmentoring.org

www.ingramcontent.com/pod-product-compliance
Lightning Source LLC
Chambersburg PA
CBHW040329300426
44113CB00020B/2694